LOVED WORKING At The CTA

The Memoirs Of

A Public Transit Train Operator

In Chicago

Marcus L. Boston

TAMPA FLORIDA

44512 BOSTON, MARCUS

ISBN: 9781959275305

LIBRARY OF CONGRESS: 2023944734

cta

UNFAZED PUBLISHING
YOUR MIND IS OUR BUSINESS

MARCUS L
BOSTON WORLD

44512 BOSTON, MARCUS

UNFAZED PUBLISHING
YOUR MIND IS OUR BUSINESS

Dedication

I dedicate this book to all of my outstanding hard working former coworkers at the Chicago Transit Authority and to some of you who have retired. The great memories I have of you are forever appreciated. No one really knows what we really deal with as public servants, but at least we had each other in the worst of times, and most of all, the best of times. We were each other's greatest strength. I write this book with love for all of you. God bless you.

Table of Contents

Chapter One	Welcome Aboard	10
Chapter Two	The Good Times	91
Chapter Three	The End Of The Line	122

About The Author

Book Me

44512 BOSTON, MARCUS

Welcome Aboard

I started the Chicago Transit Authority April 10th, 2006. Our class began at 567 W. Lake Street. I was very excited about having a good job. I was the only person in our class asking lots of questions about all of the paperwork we had to sign. I only knew one person in our class. We both went to the same church. Everyone in this class was open to talking and getting to know each other. We were soon joking and laughing before we were assigned to our home terminals. We were all full time Combined Rail Operators and so happy to learn about CTA trains.

I remember the first time I had to step over the 3rd rail. The 3rd rail is the elevated track which is electrified to power the train. It's adjacent to the rails the wheels of the train move upon. Falling on this rail can be deadly. I was shaking in fear and laughing at the same time. Our instructor was laughing too as she said, "If you fall on it you have 6 seconds to live. I'll have to kick you off of it. This is why we wear leather shoes and boots. Step over it…" I lifted up my right leg and stepped over the

3rd rail very carefully. Now it was between both of my legs and I was more terrified as I laughed in fear. My classmates were laughing with me and several more were scared with me. I was so relieved after I crossed it. I was taught that day to always respect the 3rd rail and never get too comfortable around it. This is how accidents happen. She informed us of the many accidents that have happened and when she was finished sharing those incidents there was only silence among us. I stood there gazing at the 3rd rail thinking of the people who came to work and didn't make it home. Our instructor broke our silence by continuing our tour of the train yard. She called my name a few times because I appeared to be disconnected from the tour. I apologized and shared my mind was still on the 3rd rail tragedies you shared. She told me to get focused on what she was saying and think about that later. It shook me that people died on the 3rd rail that worked at the CTA.

Four weeks later our class was assigned to our home terminals. I was assigned to 95th Red Line

Terminal. I was told the Red Line was a tough line to work and if you could work the Red Line you could work any line. Well, I was still new to Chicago. I moved to Chicago from Tampa Florida in August 2003. I was born in Chicago, but moved to Tampa with my mom at age 16. I'm a black man who wasn't used to living in the hood anymore. I was used to living in multicultural communities. I had friends in many different nationalities in Tampa. Now I was back in Chicago and living in a black neighborhood. One day I asked my mom, "Where are all the white people? Where are the Asians and Latinos?" She started laughing at me. I was serious. Nonetheless, there I was on the Red Line "ready to provide our customers with excellent service." This was something I started saying to my coworkers, along with a few other sayings like, "Thank you for working at the CTA." Thus, the title of this book.

Before I had a train by myself I was a student operator. The training train was not a good experience. Our instructors were very mean. Those first 2 days had us very insecure about being train operators. We had some very good line instructors on day 3. I spoke on behalf of our entire class. I was very sincere and told them what happened to all of us. This day was far better than the 2 previous days. They were outstanding! We student operators all became secure and confident enough to continue on to the next level.

After we completed the training train, we were assigned to operators who would further train us as they worked on the Red Line. All of the operators were awesome. I didn't have any complications, no arguments, and no conflicts of any kind. Most of these operators who trained me are now retired. I had a great time learning from them and they taught me many things I didn't learn on the training train. My first operator asked me to watch her as she operated and copy how she operated. One particular operator showed me some things the other operators didn't show me. I absorbed everything. I learned quicker ways to operate the train and I was told better ways to trouble shoot. I was very happy operating the train and this carried on after I was a qualified train operator by myself.

My first night on my first train I was very nervous. I looked at my first schedule which was on an overnight shift. I believed my run sheet said my train departed at 10:20pm, but I read my schedule wrong. It was actually 8:20pm. So I'm at home watching television and my cellphone rings. "Mr. Boston where are you?" I answer, "I'm at home watching tv. How are you tonight?" They respond, "You're supposed to be here right now Mr. Boston." I was confused as I uttered, "No I'm not. My train leaves at 10:20pm." She started laughing and I could hear more laughter in the background. Apparently I was on speaker phone. Then I could hear them talking to each other for a moment. She gets back on the phone, "Mr. Boston your train is scheduled to leave right now. You read your schedule wrong…" I was still confused as I interrupted her, "… That's not true. I have my schedule right here. It says… Oh my God! OH MY GOD!!!..." She started laughing along with those who were in the background. "…I'M ON MY WAY RIGHT NOW! I AM SO SORRY! OH MY GOD!..." I heard more laughter and then, "Mr. Boston your train just left without you. We put someone on "show up" on it. What time will you be here?..." We went from there. I came to work feeling terrible that I was late for my very first train. When I arrived my manager says in front of the clerk, "Mr. Boston we are not going to write you up for this. We believe you sincerely read your schedule wrong. When your train returns you'll take over." I was overjoyed. I waited until my train returned and the person on "show up" was happy they got to do one trip and go home.

My first train from 95th to Howard was exciting and scary at the same time. I was extra nice and polite to everyone. I had no issues of any kind on my first night and I was happy to be operating a train. I would sing railroad songs and cartoon songs while I operated. "I've been working on the railroad. All the long long day. I am moving all these passengers for the CTA." Then I would laugh to myself. "Charlie says. Love my Good & Plenty. Charlie says. Really rings a bell. Charlie says. Love my Good & Plenty. Don't know any other candy that I love so well." Then I would add, "Good & Plenty Good & Plenty Good & Plenty." I had so much fun singing these railroad songs and making up songs as I operated. I didn't realize this would become the norm for me, and I also started praying as I operated. When I upgraded my cellphone I started playing music. There was no 0 cellphone policy during this time.

I wasn't the best operator when I first began operating. One day I had a manager who was on my train. When they got off they said it wasn't a smooth ride and that I was terrible. This was discouraging. I struggled on my midnight schedule, but the Control Center was very understanding. I recall when I couldn't open the "Modesty Panel." This is a compartment that was outside of the motor cab (area where I operate) by door number 2. My train started malfunctioning and I needed to open it so I could troubleshoot. The Controller was pleasant as they instructed me on what to do. This Controller was very mellow at all times. Oftentimes he would announce the exact CTA time on the radio. I soon made sure my watch was set to the time he announced. I always checked my watch when he made this announcement. I missed him when he retired. A few Controllers kept up his tradition, but many others didn't. The instructions he gave to enter the modesty panel worked and I thanked him so much. I literally felt like a child in that moment northbound at Wilson. The old wood Wilson station. During my time as a student operator I didn't experience any train break downs. Even though this was good this was also bad. I needed to experience this with an operator so I could see them troubleshooting, and so I could see how they communicate on the CTA radio. I needed to see them handle the pressure from the train riders being frustrated. I needed to see angry riders and riders who would yell at you. I didn't experience any of this while I was a student operator.

As I continued working those midnight shifts I

started experiencing the negative side of being a train operator. My respectful attitude wasn't considered by the angry riders or the homeless people that didn't want to get off at Howard. I called my supervisor on short range radio informing her of my situation. Her reply, "Operator 956 you're too nice. You have to be mean if you want them to get up." I didn't want to be mean or disrespectful, but I tried it. I screamed at the top of my lungs in a mean manner and they got up. Some exited quietly and others cursed me out as they exited, but it worked. As the months passed by I grew tired of being like this. I went back to being nice and polite, but with the knowledge that I can get security. I said things like, "Excuse me sir (or ma'am). You're at Howard. This train is out of service. You must exit." Some cursed me out and others acted as if they were still asleep. I replied, "I'm being nice. Now those that will come to get you off this train will not be nice." They refused to leave and when security came, or the police, they got up quickly. I appreciated the security at Howard Terminal. They were regulars and I soon got to know them better than some of my CTA coworkers. On the flip side, there were many homeless that appreciated my kindness and respect towards them. These are the homeless people that I started to get to know. I soon helped them with cash, in winter I gave them my gloves, and sometimes my lunch on occasion.

As I got to know the regular homeless riders my heart went out to them. There were these 2 homeless sisters who rode my train. I couldn't believe my eyes when I saw them the first time. I was so shocked I took a picture. Again, there was no 0 cellphone policy at this time. I felt so bad these 2 grey haired sisters were homeless. I wondered if they had family or children they could stay with. I was disturbed every time I saw them on my train or on CTA property. Here's the photo I took. They pushed these bags and their bag amount grew as the years went by. I remember the time when I saw them both without their bags. I knew something bad took place. I didn't bother asking. By the time I resigned from CTA one of the sister's died and the

other was living at the CTA bus stop at 87th street next to the Dan Ryan Expressway.

There was a homeless man that died who rode my train regularly. Unfortunately this man smelled unbelievably bad. He was tall. I believe 6 foot 4 or 5. He was a skinny man and walked with a limp. The last time I saw him alive was when I arrived at Howard Terminal and left my train on track 4. I smelled a horrible smell and asked, “What is that?” A platform coworker pointed inside my train. It was the 3rd or 4th rail car. I couldn’t believe my eyes. It was the skinny homeless man. However, he looked terrible. His head was leaning on the train window as he sat in the middle of the rail car. There was snot hanging from his nose. Several inches of it just hanging. I was disgusted at the sight. I immediately thought, [Omg! He's sick!] I was told to go to another train, and didn't have time to go to the atm. I had to take a train out immediately back to 95th because of delays. When I got off work that night I went to the atm and took out 60 dollars. I was going to give it to the homeless man so he could buy some over the counter medicine, and a cheap motel room. That was the last of my money, but I wanted him to have it. I've never considered what homeless people do when they get sick. I was so hurt to see him like this. The next day I kept asking my coworkers about him. I was looking for him and didn't see him. I kept asking my coworkers until I received bad news. He was found dead on the train. I was stunned and the news didn't process until I was operating my train. I started crying over this man and put the 60 dollars back into my wallet on my lunch. I had the money in my pocket ready to give it to him quickly when I finally saw him. What a lonely death and I have never forgotten him.

Another homeless man died, but his death wasn't

because of illness. Allegedly he fell down the stairs at Howard Terminal and broke his neck. I found this hard to believe. There were no cameras at Howard during this time. This homeless man's name was Kevin, or was it Keith? This man was a regular. I got to talk with him many times and plenty of my coworkers knew him by name. This man would cause so many delays by holding doors (keeping a train door open preventing the train from moving), or pulling doors (There's an emergency pull lever above CTA train doors that opens the rail car door, and causes the train to stop accelerating. Which in turn makes us apply the brakes. Once the train is stopped we checked our train to manually close the open door. If the train is standing still the train will not move until the door is closed.). He would pull a door open and run to another adjacent train. We also had solicitors who did this as well, but Kevin/Keith was a real nuisance. I remember when he pulled the doors on a Purple Line train. He got off the train at the old Wilson station on the island. The island was a section between the Purple Line track 4 and Red

Line on track 3 northbound. There were no exits on the island. I never knew its purpose. It wasn't for customer use. He refused to get back on the train and I knew the Controller was going to call me. Yep, Control called me, "Control to the train leaving Sheridan northbound?" I responded. "Your message Control." "Can you please see if you could get the man to board your train?" "10-4 Control." I replied. I stopped my train and pulled a single door open in my head car. He looked at me as I said, "C'mon." He got on my train without incident. I was very good to him through the years I knew him. I gave him money, gloves, food, and we shared several conversations. We were the same age, but he looked so much older. He had a big belly and most of his hair was grey. He ended up homeless because his girlfriend kicked him out. He burned many bridges with his family and had nowhere to go. I was saddened hearing how he died. He knew CTA property very well and I personally believed someone pushed him or purposely tripped him as he ran down the stairs. Many of my coworkers and I talked about this the next day at work. Not one of us believed he tripped or fell down the stairs. Keith / Kevin had lots of people who hated the delays he caused daily. Then again, maybe he did fall. We will never know.

From my first year to year number 4, I experienced many hard things. Trains breaking down happened often, but I remember my first morning rush hour. It was on my day off. I received a call from the clerk asking me if I was interested in working. I agreed to come in. I was talking with the supervisor at 95th prior to boarding my train. There was an emergency going on and the radios were very busy. When I boarded my train I was already 10 minutes late. When I arrived at 79th Street station northbound, I opened the doors so my riders could exit and new riders could board. After everyone boarded I closed the doors of my train. However, the panel on my train had an indication that there was a door still open. The airways were still very busy with the previous emergency and we didn't have CTA work issued cellphones at this time. As time ticked on I started to panic and I was sweating. Angry riders sounded off one after another, “I have to get to work.” , “Damn! Hurry the fuck up!” , and “Are you dumb? Fix this train! I need to get to the airport!” I opened and closed the doors several times hoping I was free to proceed. Each time I did this more and more people ran to the train as the CTA buses arrived outside. The Control center didn’t have the better system they have now and there were no train monitoring systems in the supervisor booths at this time. I had one of the old 2600 trains with no cameras or digital signs. Control called me when the emergency ended, “Operator northbound at 79th? Why are you standing?” This began our radio back and forth. By the time Control called me I had checked my train and all doors were closed although my panel said a door was still open. Train malfunctions really suck in the morning rush. With me still being a new operator and very nervous, I used the wrong CTA radio code. As the Controller gave me instructions on how to move the train she added, “What are y'all teaching these new operators?" Long range radio transmissions are heard by everyone on that specific channel, and sometimes on shared multiple channels. I ended up going express and had to pick up a manager. This manager went off on me because I used the wrong radio code. I tried to explain myself, but he got more aggressive. This is when I learned to just shut up and not defend myself with managers. The manager took over my train as he continued yelling at me. They wanted to put me into retraining because they thought my train stood there more than 10 minutes. Fortunately for me the 95th supervisor called Control and the managers saying I left 95th 10 minutes late. The manager got off my train at Belmont and I took the train to Howard. Even though I was significantly late, I still had 25 minutes before my train was scheduled to depart. I appreciated this very much. Years later that recover time was eliminated. Too many times when I was significantly late, as soon as I arrived at Howard, I had to leave right out immediately. I hated when we lost our recovery time. There was no time to unwind from the stress. Anyway, during this recover time, I grabbed a snack at the store downstairs inside Howard Terminal and went to the CTA ready room for operators near the supervisor booth. As I walked in they were talking about me and the wrong CTA radio codes I used. They had too many jokes. Finally one operator pointed at me, "What's your run number? (I answered 918.) Ohhhhh, that was you!!!" Everyone exploded into laughter causing me to exit. I sat on a bench on the old wooden platform and waited to be called by the Howard supervisor. I felt down being the butt of many jokes. I had yet to achieve a sense of humor with CTA dilemmas. It took me many years to see the bright side of the bad things that happened at work.

I continued having bad days at work over the next several years. These situations broke me in thoroughly into a Chicagoan. That Tampa side of me began to decline. As I began to witness fights, robberies, foolishness, ignorance, and nastiness, my personality adjusted. My skin became thick.

Because I lived in a multicultural community in Tampa, I didn't witness the things I experienced on the Red Line. It broke my heart and I won't share anything specific. I grew tired of filling out paperwork at the end of my shifts when I just wanted to go home. There were days when I had to relax and shake the work day off before I went home. Days like this continued even until I resigned. However, I really hated when my train had to stand waiting for the police to arrive. I knew there was at least one person on my train who didn't have time to stand still. They needed every minute to get where they were going. On delays where I had to give my train riders "Train Delay Slips," angry riders let me have it. Some riders were in tears because they couldn't afford to be late again. I prayed for these riders and hoped their job understood. I know CTA was understanding if we rode CTA to work. We weren't in trouble if the train or bus broke down or if the train or bus was late.

I was happy when the Chicago Police arrived

quickly and disappointed when they arrived late. I loved when criminals were caught and hated when they got away. I've been robbed before and it's not a pleasant experience. It's very traumatic. At least it was for me believing they were going to pull the trigger. They didn't kill me and I was grateful. I filed a police report and later cried about it. As I continued having days where I needed the police, I began being just as angry as my riders. There was something about me being just as angry that made my riders be at peace with me. They were happy I sincerely cared about their situation and their money. I didn't want anyone late to work because of foolishness on my train.

My good regular riders were a joy to see. I looked forward to seeing them daily. Whenever I didn't see them on the train platform I waited an extra minute and most times there they came running. Sometimes their bus was late. As I learned how CTA functioned it made me a better operator for my good regular riders. Before CTA enforced all of the rules, I admit, I broke the rules. Not purposely. I never read the entire CTA Rule Book. I read all the serious rules and neglected the rest. I was informed to read it many times. I would ride with the door open and talked to my regular riders and my friends as I operated. I was having a good time having these conversations. I didn't know that was a safety violation. I was having a good time in my ignorance. It caught up to me though. You'll read about that a little later.

Working overnight was a lot of fun because there were no managers and spotters riding the train. Spotters were people who worked for CTA who wore regular clothing. They looked like regular riders. When ever we broke a CTA rule or had a safety violation, if a Spotter witnessed it they reported the incident. Many of us had to see our manager because of Spotters. The Spotter didn't have to be present when we had to see our manager. The key words I learned that meant a Spotter reported me was when a manager said the following, "It was brought to our attention that you did..." Or, "Someone witnessed you doing such and such…" No one ever had a name of the person who reported us. It was our word against theirs, but their word was practically law. Because the 2600, 2200, and 2400 series trains didn't have cameras, we had no evidence to fight against the Spotters report. Once we had the new 5000 series train, the cameras either confirmed what the Spotter reported or it showed that Spotter wasn't correct. Cameras got me out of trouble many times. When I talked with my coworkers about Spotters, many of them said I was crazy. They didn't believe me. That's was ok. I soon learned to be quiet about Spotters.

Even as I appreciated seeing my good regular riders, I didn't appreciate seeing regular trouble making riders. Customer Assistants (CA) would call me on short range radio telling me if a troublemaker boarded my train. When I worked as a CA I did the same. I always appreciated a heads up. Here's one example of the bad regular riders. On Saturday evening around 8pm I arrived at Chicago / State on the Red Line southbound. Every week there was a group of teenagers who started fights. I could never make it to Roosevelt (6 stations later) before I had to call for Chicago Police assistance. After 4 straight weeks of this I would call CTA Control to inform them they were boarding my train before the fights started. The regular Controller understood my call, but when I had other Controllers, I was asked to only call if I had an emergency. For 6 straight weeks I needed police assistance. Week number 7 was the beginning of peace. The police were present at Chicago when my train arrived and those teenagers didn't start any trouble. The police boarded my train and rode with those teens. I was so happy and they did this every week until those teenagers didn't board my train anymore. It took several weeks to pass by before I stopped looking for them to board my train.

As I continued to gain experience as a train operator, one particular night changed me forever. I was entering the Sheridan station northbound around 3am. After I berthed my train and opened the doors, the police ran up the stairs asking me to leave my doors open. They searched my train and asked me who boarded. I told them the truth. I wasn't looking at the people on the platform. They looked so disappointed and one of them replied, "You weren't paying attention?" They walked off. I watched them as they walked away from me. I kept the doors open and one of them turned around to say, "You can close your doors and proceed." This situation made me feel bad. I was trained to look out for the marker as I entered the station. I never looked at the people on the platform. I never knew why the police wanted me to keep my doors open. Maybe a criminal got away. Because of this incident I started looking at the people on the platforms as I berthed my train. On the overnight shift there weren't many people to see. The next time the police asked me who boarded my train I could tell them what they had on and which rail car they boarded. Sometimes people would walk through the train to other rail cars causing us to search the whole train to find them. I was always happy to help the police. I tried to be a Chicago Police Officer, but I failed the exam by a few points. I also tried to be an Evanston Police Officer. Evanston is a suburb just north of Chicago. I passed all of their exams, I passed the lie detector, I passed the psychiatric evaluation, and passed their physical tests. However, the city of Evanston turned down my application because I didn't have a security guard background and because I didn't have a Criminal Justice degree. I was so disappointed. I appealed their decision and they turned me down again.

As I began to pay attention to the people on the platform, I began to identify behavior patterns. Regular riders when they exited the train would walk away from my line of sight so I could see clearly. I appreciated them for this. I noticed that regular riders got in place to board the train. No one watched me at all. When my close friends were on the platform preparing to board, I saw them, but they didn't see me. Once my head was outside of my window I called them to get their attention. It was amazing that people didn't watch me at all. As I continued paying attention to platform patterns, I clearly saw the Spotters. I wasn't crazy. Here's what I did. After I berthed my train, I opened my window slowly, and looked around briefly before I opened my train doors. It was in this moment where I saw the Spotters. They were the only people looking at me. Regular riders were facing the train and got angry if the doors didn't open quick enough for them. Lol. Most train operators didn't look around. Just like the regular riders facing the train was normal, it was normal for train operators to only watch the doors of the train open and close. No train operators looked around. As I began looking around I saw those who were looking at me. When I looked at them they looked away. I told my fellow train operators this information. They had all kinds of jokes and comments about me. "You don't see Spotters." "It's all in your head." "Ain't nobody watching you." I was stunned so many didn't believe me. As the years passed by and I began to have my own "Student Train Operators" assigned to me, I taught them to look around for suspicious activity. I taught them to observe their surroundings and pay attention. After the Blue Line Ohare incident, Spotters were now everywhere and during all shifts. The entire platform changed from what used to be normal. I noticed it immediately. Everyone didn't face the train anymore. There were groups of two or more that always had one person facing me directly. I thought, "Are they watching me?" And they were watching me. People with smart phones stood at an angle with their phone turned to the side. This was so odd. The first time this happened I said to myself, "Are they watching me?" I even waved my hand at them which caused them to flinch. Then it happened again at the next station. When this happened again I knew I wasn't crazy. Honestly I hated Spotters because I looked at them as professional snitches. I understood why CTA hired them, but I still didn't like it.

It's true that I broke many safety rules to get my riders to their stations as quickly as I could. Some rules I wasn't aware of and didn't even know I was breaking the rules. Like I said before, I was instructed and taught to read the entire CTA Rule Book, but I didn't. Well, one day a CTA Instructor boarded my train in the State Street Subway. I was completely myself as they entered my Motor Cab. She introduced herself. She was no nonsense, but I was full of nonsense. I loved joking around and didn't stop although an Instructor was watching me operate. This Instructor was shocked at what I was doing and told me boldly, "What!? You're going to do that right in front of me!" I responded to her feeling confused, "Do what? What are you talking about?" "What am I talking about? You're breaking rules in front of me! I should write you up! How dare you?!" She replied feeling as if I was disrespecting her. I really didn't know what she was talking about because I didn't read the CTA Rule Book. I wasn't upset, mad, or offended at all as she explained everything I was doing wrong and I had better stop doing it immediately. I listened to her and she was satisfied to see me putting her instruction into immediate action. She had mercy on me. She told me to read the entire CTA Rule Book and I said I would. I was so grateful she boarded my train that day. I read the entire CTA Rule Book and learned many things I was guilty of doing. I literally had to consciously practice operating because the things I was doing wrong were really rooted in my train operations. This CTA Instructor boarded my train every two weeks it seemed. Each time she witnessed improvement and she was pleased I listened to her. She also started asking me questions from the CTA Rule Book and I answered her questions correctly. She smiled at me. This was a very pleasant sight to see because she was so no nonsense as she watched me operate my train. As months passed by, I could finally joke and operate my train per the CTA Rule Book. When the new CTA Trains arrived, the 5000 series, everything changed. These trains had cameras that recorded everything. Then CTA added cameras inside the Motor Cab which recorded us operating the train. This was so uncomfortable for me. It felt like someone was standing over me watching. It took me a long time to adjust to this new way of operating.

I really appreciated that Instructor because some operators were being wrote up based on the recordings. I was so happy I no longer broke rules. My regular riders recognized the difference in how I operated my train. Some complained saying I was now a slow operator. I explained to them this is how CTA desires me to operate. They were not happy. Some operators were fired based on the things they did while operating. I hated when our company made the news or another transit train company made the news. We all understood new safety rules were coming. When the female train operator who was on her mobile phone, crashed into the train ahead of her and died, we knew drastic changes were going to be made. She worked in another city, but they had a similar train safety system to ours. Yep, no more mobile phones while we operated our trains. I hated I couldn't play my music anymore. It made my day more peaceful listening to jazz or gospel music. All of a sudden CTA had mobile phones for us to use in case of emergency. This was a good idea and a bad idea in my opinion. On one hand, we could call in emergencies if the radio airways were busy, but on the other hand, we had to bring our train to a complete stop before we could make a call on our mobile phone. There was one particular night when the radio wasn't working or no one was listening. I'm not sure. I had an emergency on my train and was calling it in on my radio as I approached Sox 35th Northbound. No one responded and the airways were not busy. Once my train was inside the station, I opened the doors. I then called my emergency in on my CTA mobile phone. I was put on hold. I hung up and called back. I was put on hold again. There was a violent act taking place involving a large group of people. I used my radio again and no one responded. I called again on my CTA mobile phone and no one picked up this time. Although I wasn't supposed to use my personal mobile phone, or have it on my person, I pulled out my mobile phone and called 9 1 1. I explained I was a CTA Red Line operator at Sox 35th etc., and two undercover police exited my train in a Chicago Cubs Jersey and a White Sox Jersey. They were somewhere in the middle of my train of 8 rail cars. They arrested most of the individuals, but some fled the scene as the Chicago Police Department (CPD) closed in on the violent act taking place. This was a 20 minute delay and I had 2 trains standing behind me outside of the station. No one called me on the radio asking why I was standing. I wasn't given an express run. No one called me on my CTA mobile phone. This situation happened at night time. When I finally proceeded from Sox 35th, as I passed by train operators I asked them on short range radio if they heard my emergency transmission. All of them said yes. When I arrived at Howard Terminal, I asked my supervisor if they heard me and they said they didn't hear me. They didn't ask me why my train was late either. I really don't know what happened that night, but I was glad I had my personal mobile phone on me. I kept it on me with the ringer off just in case this happened again.

I didn't share this to make my former employer

look bad. Things happen all the time when you have a 24 hour, 7 days a week, 365 days a year transit system that never closes. The Red Line and Blue Line were always open. Trains breakdown and radio systems break down. Mobile phone calls fail and sometimes have no signal or a weak signal. People call off of work. One night when I was working, most of the train operators called off. There were only 4 trains in operation between 95th and Howard during the evening. They were 30 minutes apart. This was terrible service. Trains should be 8 to 10 minutes apart. After this took place CTA started moving people who could operate a train from other duties, and made them operate the train so riders wouldn't be inconvenienced. I hated this personally, but I also understood why. I could be working as a Flagman, a Customer Assistant, or a Switchman, and then they tell me I had to take a train out. Sometimes we had to pick the train up from various locations. One example of this was when I wasn't feeling well and I called it in. CTA had a Customer Assistant take over my train southbound at 47th

Street Station. An ambulance took me to the hospital from 47th while the Customer Assistant took my train to 95th. Can you imagine if the train just sat there with no one to take over? I'm sure the Customer Assistant wasn't happy, but I was grateful to get to the hospital in a timely manner. I was diagnosed with Bell's Palsy. The entire right side of my face was paralyzed.

Like I was saying, things happen at CTA and things malfunction all the time. The signal lights breakdown. The Towers which Control the signals malfunction. Entire Intersections stop working. The train tracks need to be repaired or replaced. Most days when there are no issues, no one says thank you or have a nice day. The few people who said these words always caught me off guard. I was grateful to hear those words. However, when delays happen we are greatly hated.

I learned that the best of Chicago rides our trains, and the worst of Chicago rides our trains. When CTA things break down and cause delays these worlds collide. Sometimes when my train broke down these worlds started arguing over me. I've seen it. The good riders defended me as the bad riders cursed me out. I learned to do my best for those who appreciated me and I had to learn to ignore the people who hated CTA although they rode with us regularly. There were times when I let being cursed out get the best of me. I would respond, "Get a car and leave us alone since you hate us so much." This only made the angry riders angrier. I've been pushed and threatened many times, but never assaulted in a manner where I needed medical assistance. However, other operators were assaulted and some needed medical assistance. Lots of bad things happen, but lots of good things happen too. It took awhile for me to enjoy the good things because I was on edge ready for the bad things to happen, and when things go wrong, even the good regular riders could release their anger in those delayed moments. I hated having a train full of angry riders. I paid close attention when riders were angry. I mentioned I've been pushed and shoved before. All professionalism went out the window in that moment. No matter how much training and preparation I may have obtained, real life real world in real time things show you exactly who you are in that moment. I was ready to fight many times. I was threatened many times. I remembered the trouble makers and my good regular riders remembered them too. It was my regular riders who stepped in on my behalf many times. Kindness goes a long way and I've always appreciated them for stepping in. I've never needed medical attention from the negative people who ride the CTA. Whenever a coworker was physically assaulted it put all CTA personnel on high alert. I know many of us have some of the worse attitudes and dispositions as CTA employees, and I'm not trying to make excuses for it, but many of us have experienced very traumatic things at work. So many different situations trigger those traumas. Fortunately for me, I pray about my CTA experiences. However, there was one time when so many different things piled up from work and my personal life that led my doctor to send me to a psychiatrist. After one sitting my psychiatrist sent me to a professional counselor. He said I didn't need his services, but he prescribed with me medication to treat depression and generalized anxiety called Lexapro. Little did I know this was the only prescription drug I could use and continue working at the CTA. My condition was bad enough that my doctor did not release me back to work for almost 8 months. When I returned to work I had to take refresher training, several exams, and perform trouble shooting in the yard. A CTA Instructor rode a train with me while I operated to make sure I know what I'm doing. Everyone at work kept asking me, "Are you ok? You're not acting like yourself." Well, Lexapro took away my personality. I was neither happy nor sad. I was numb. I could hear the funniest joke and keep a straight face. I was asked, "Why don't you find this joke funny?" I would answer, "It is funny." When things happened on my train I had no emotional response. I called in fights and handled major train break downs with the greatest of ease. Although I was productively functional, I hated that I was numb. I didn't like this feeling. I kept asking my doctor to take me off of Lexapro and he insisted I stay on it. On the other hand, I enjoyed my weekly counseling sessions. Although I was on Lexapro I was able to open up and share my experiences. He was a very good counselor. I say this because during my time on Lexapro I didn't open up to those who were closest to me. I enjoyed being alone. I didn't want to hangout or go anywhere. When I was finally off of Lexapro, it took a while before my personality returned. I was weaned off of it with lower doses until my doctor finally said I didn't need it anymore. I was never the same operator after counseling. I handled serious situations without my emotions getting the best of me. CTA has a program for us to talk and receive counseling. I can't think of the name of it, but I did use it some years later after my Lexapro experience. I was on the platform at Howard Terminal when I heard gun shots. I strongly yelled for everyone to move to the end of the northbound platform. I reported the situation and checked the area once the shots stopped. I then advised the Control Center. There was a young man bleeding on our platform. He was shot in the stairwell leading upstairs to the northbound platform. I was walking by this stairwell when the shots were fired. It didn't take long for the Chicago Police and medical to arrive. Fortunately for this young man, there was a nurse and a doctor on the platform with the things they needed to stop his bleeding. They worked on him until medical arrived. I stood several feet nearby praying for this young man. There was another individual standing near me and I later talked with them. They were also praying for the young man. After the young man was transported to a local hospital, we were informed that he didn't make it. CTA sent a trauma counselor to Howard and I was very pleased to talk with this person. I knew from experience to open up and talk about it. There was so much blood. I remember his eyes. They were full of terror. After he was transported I remembered the blood that remained on the platform. The gauze which were used to stop his bleeding remained and some blew onto the tracks. I notified the cleanup crew up. As the cleanup sanitized the platform and tracks, I recognized an emotion I had before. In this moment I started thinking, "No one from CTA called me to see if I was ok. No one asked if I needed medical." Someone was talking on the radio asking if any CTA employees were still on the platform. I responded and my emotions were starting to get the best of me. When management arrived I was free to go. As I entered Howard Terminal break room, I was surprised to see a trauma counselor. I was happy to see their presence and went straight to them. I was right on time as they began talking to us about this incident. I asked questions and learned many more things about trauma. I purposely do not desire to add this information to this book. After they completed talking to us, I took the time to talk one on one with them. I needed it. Once again my personal life added to my emotional state being that my marriage was in serious trouble. I needed this talk and the information I received. I was so happy I talked to the trauma counselor. Most of the things that happen on our job never make the news. There are things I remember that I would never write in this book and if you interview me about it, I will not tell you. Don't ask! This situation made the news and I always hated when we made the news for something negative.

I've been on the news several times because of things that happened with my train. Of course my face and identity was never disclosed, but my heart went out to my coworkers who had their identities released to the public. I don't want to be specific because I do not desire to bring any more attention to their lives that have been changed forever. However, one of them I related to because their circumstance could have been mine. The scenario surrounding their train incident I was guilty of many times. So many times I found myself in their exact same situation, but I never had their result. I've prayed in tears for them many times for their well-being.

I mentioned that I made the news before. I'll

share my train incidents that made the news. The first time my train made the news was when I was on an express run from Sox 35th to Jackson northbound in the subway. I was at 25mph in coast as I passed Roosevelt and once my 8 car train passed Roosevelt, I tried to accelerate my speed. I immediately noticed my train didn't respond. I pulled the curtain back and saw only the CTA emergency lights on. I put my train back in coast because I was on a downhill grade approaching Harrison station. I called Control, "Operator (number) northbound approaching Harrison Control." Control responded, "Your message." "My train has no power. Is the power off?" I asked and Control looked in it. I passed Harrison and stayed in coast on the downhill grade. I made it to Jackson while Control, supervisors, and managers were all working together to see why there was no power. The customer assistant at Roosevelt was asked to help. Meanwhile I was instructed to inform my riders my train was out of service because the power was out. This occurred in the heart of the evening rush hour and my train was packed. I made my announcement. My riders exited the station to catch a bus or to go to our upstairs trains on the Chicago Loop. As I was searching my train, there was a woman sitting alone on one of my rail cars. I opened the door and I was informing her the train was out of service. She responded with sign language. I made sure to face her and allow her to read my lips. She was somewhat older and didn't understand me. I suppose I was not pronouncing my words correctly. I had a girlfriend who was deaf and I remember a few things she taught me to do to communicate. I walked her off my train and allowed her to see everyone was gone. I pointed and gestured best I could until she nodding like "Ohhhhhhhhh." I didn't want to give her the wrong directions so I walked her upstairs and outside of Jackson station. I walked with her until she was at the stairs going up to CTA Adams / Wabash Station on the Chicago Loop. She smiled and mouthed thank you with her sign. I told her she was welcome. I returned to my train and made sure it was completely empty with the "Out Of Service" signs. Control called me and asked me to walk the tracks back towards Roosevelt. I had my CTA vest on and searched the tracks with my flash light. As I passed Harrison station the customer assistant at Roosevelt called Control, "CA at Roosevelt to Control." Control responded "Your message CA at Roosevelt." CA says, "Control, the 3rd rail is laying flat on the ground Control." Now I was halfway to Roosevelt when Control called me and told me to return to my train because management was looking for me. I didn't know I was on the news until management took me to a CTA vehicle outside of Jackson station. I had to talk with CTA persons I've never seen before. All I did was tell the truth. There wasn't much to tell. "I was on an express run and I was in coast. Then the power went out. I called Control and informed them." It was an open and shut case. The subway was closed northbound and all the trains behind me had to be rerouted over the Chicago Loop train tracks. I wasn't in trouble and didn't need to be disciplined because it wasn't my fault the 3rd rail fell over.

Another time my train made the news was northbound at Loyola. As my train departed Granville station I had 2 defects at the same time that registered on my panel. I looked outside my window to see if my train had any smoke and I clearly saw it. The CTA radio was busy with another emergency so I called it in on my CTA mobile phone. I made an announcement that we were experiencing an equipment problem and began troubleshooting. I was glad the problem was in my 2nd car within my 8 car consist. After I entered the 2nd car, I quickly saw that the lights and the emergency lights were off. This caught my attention along with black smoke inside the rail car. I cut out the motors in the 2nd car which should make the smoke stop and planned to return to my motor cab. I tried to close the door that I opened, but it wouldn't close. This made me greatly concerned. The lights were off, the emergency lights were off, and now the door wouldn't close. It was as if the door didn't have any power. The CTA radio was still busy with the other emergency. I was quite calm as I returned to my motor cab. I tried to close all the doors in my train consist, but the door which didn't close did not respond, and the other door didn't move either. I went back to my 2nd car and noticed the smoke did not thin. I asked everyone inside the 2nd car to exit to my head car because of the smoke.

When I returned to my motor cab I looked outside my window and the smoke did not dissipate. I grabbed my intercom headset and said, "Attention CTA riders. I would like everyone to exit this train for safety reasons while I attempt to correct the issue. Please exit this train until I know it's safe. Thank you." I had a deadhead crew on my train. A deadhead crew is an on duty employee who can assist if needed. Deadhead crews ride from Terminal to Terminal. My deadhead crew called me on short range radio. He asked if I needed assistance. I declined, but said thanks. I called Control on my CTA mobile to give an update, and then I decided to check my train at track level. When I arrived at my second car I couldn't believe my eyes. My train was on fire. I called my deadhead crew on short range and told him the train is on fire, and I'm about to call Control. He responded, "10-4 Marcus. I'll walk the rider's downstairs because they are going to route around us." "10-4 (I said his name.) I called Control on long range radio saying 10-99. This is the call code you never want to hear on the radio. Everyone will shut up and let you talk after saying this code. "Control. I'm requesting the power be removed northbound at Loyola. I have a 10-80 train." Control responded strongly, "I HOPE YOU EVACUATED YOUR TRAIN OPERATOR!" I was very calm when I said, "Control, the train is evacuated and my deadhead crew is walking the rider's downstairs to street level." When Control said, "EXCELLENT WORK!" I wanted to record my train burning on my cellphone lol. My train looked as if it was on a rotisserie. There was a blue flame that burned on a big pipe looking thing in the middle of my train. When I heard the power go off, the flames dissipated almost instantly. CTA crews arrived moments later and they did all the work. I observed and took notes. The Chicago Fire Department (CFD) arrived and I was happy they didn't need to do anything. The train was empty and the riders were already downstairs. When I got home around 4 in the morning, I saw my train on the news. A CTA spokesperson said, "CFD arrived. Evacuated the train, the platform, and the station. No injuries were involved." I felt some type of way about this. CFD had nothing to do, but the spokesperson said they did our CTA job in a nutshell. The spokesperson never talked to me at Loyola. Why couldn't they say what they knew? Our employees evacuated the train and the platform prior to CFD arriving. Can we get some credit? Before I knew my train was burning I asked everyone to step off the train. My deadhead walked them downstairs. Why couldn't CTA say this? I felt unappreciated.

When this incident occurred I was no longer out of 95th Terminal. I was bumped to Howard Terminal during our system pick. I picked to stay at 95th, and when the system pick was over, I was the absolute last person on the list. I was at the bottom. Something happened and we had to have another system pick immediately. I knew I wasn't going to stay at 95th being at the bottom. I picked 95th as my first option, and Howard was my second option. I ended up at Howard, and I began to love Howard Terminal. Not at first though. I used to keep to myself at first. I ended up opening up again and I'm glad I did. I stayed at Howard until I resigned.

Every CTA train operator has a day that will go down in the history of their CTA career as the worst day they ever had at work. Well, my worst CTA day was on St. Patrick's Day March 17th, 2012. The weather was 82 degrees in Chicago. It's still winter time, but not on this day. It seemed like all cultures of people rode our trains on this day. I left Howard having a midday schedule with no clue I was going to hate I came to work. By the time I got to Granville my train was packed. A fight broke out in my head car. I called Control. The fight that began on my train ended on the platform at Granville. The two men began wrestling on the ground and rolled into the train that was leaving Granville northbound. I'm calling the operator to stop their train, but they didn't stop in time. They rolled into the moving train and one of the guys back made contact with the train. Now I had to wait for medical attention to arrive. After a twenty minute delay I continued. Then there was another fight, and another fight, and another, and another, and another. It was unbelievable. On my last trip to 95th I had an all out brawl southbound at 47th street. In my 2nd car there was a fight in the middle of the train by all males. Women stood up in all the seats as if they were in an arena. When I called it in I was clearly depleted and Control responded in a very tender way. I was on the radio all day with fights and it seemed like no one else called in anything. Maybe they did. I had no recovery time. I was late for my lunch and didn't have much time to eat. This last fight had about 20 people fighting. I told Control there are too many to count and tell CPD to bring a paddy wagon. The rest of what happened at 47th I won't write in this book. When I finally arrived at 95th I dreaded taking a train back to Howard Terminal. At least my day would be over once I arrived at Howard, but I was so exhausted. Then the 95th supervisor called me on short range radio saying, "Operator 8??, do you need to use the restroom?" I replied, "No." "Ok. Stay abound this train. Have a good night." The 95th supervisor stated. "10-4. Thank you." I replied. I shut down my train and immediately the new operator energized the same train on the opposite end. I did not trim my motor cab. I kept the door locked because I didn't want to be bothered with any riders. I cried because I was so happy I didn't have to operate the train back to Howard. I was still on duty. I had one of the sweetest things happen to me. It's called "The Unscheduled Deadhead." Meaning it's not on our regular train schedule. I turned my radio off although I knew I was supposed to leave it on. When I arrived at Howard I sat down after signing out. I didn't fill out an overtime slip. I rested my mind as I prepared to go home. This day I'll never forget. I got up and went home. Once I sat down in my car I realized I forgot to fill out the paperwork for each incident on my train today. I couldn't do it. I couldn't go back to Howard to fill it out. I went home. I never filled out the paperwork for all of those fights and I was pleased the managers never asked me about the reports I never wrote.

Before I was bumped to Howard, I had a bad day I thought was my worst when I was still out of 95th. This was a night when CTA made the news downtown Chicago. The subway was closed for repairs and upgrades. All Red Line trains used the Chicago Loop elevated tracks. Well, a fire broke out on the Chicago Loop that blocked Red Line trains from getting to 95th. I was the only train between 95th and Cermak China Town. When I arrived at 95th my day was over. I could go home. When I Arrived at 95th, the supervisor called me to come see him. I responded, "Negative. I'm going home." He responded, "Negative. Come see me." I went to see him and he uttered, "I'm implementing CTA Emergency protocols, and you have to stay." He explained the rules which I already read in the CTA

Rule book. There were no more operators. I was the only one. I energized the train and took it to Cermak. At Cermak my train was out of service and I went back to 95th. I kept going back and forth for almost 2 hours. Once trains were allowed to go to 95th, I was released to go home. This night was nothing like St. Patrick's Day. I've never had another day remotely close to St. Patrick's Day.

I've also had some weird things that happened during my years at CTA. I remember when I received a call on my radio as I arrived at Sox 35th, and I responded. Then Control added, "Operator only respond to your Controller." I was baffled. Well, it turns out someone had a CTA radio and was giving instructions and orders that were not authorized by the CTA. This happened, I think, over several weeks until he was caught. The customer assistant at Jackson saw this person and reported the sighting. The guy was arrested.

On a Saturday night while arriving at Harrison in the subway. This situation happened on a very peaceful night. A very quiet night. The CTA radios were silent. I loved when the radios were silent. I had to keep checking my radio to make sure it was turned on. All was well until I was arriving into Harrison. I entered Harrison at 35 mph with my train braking and slowing down to berth. When suddenly, BOOM!!! My train remained in brake as I pulled my window back, and looked at the rear of my train consist. There was a huge cloud of smoke! I said vocally, "NO! NO!!! NO!!!!!!" As I approached the 8th car marker, I lost my power control relay. The power control relay is the safety mechanism associated with the doors. Someone opened the doors while my train was still moving. As my train came to a complete stop, people were running past me screaming toward Polk Street exit opposite of Harrison. As I walked over to open my doors, most of the doors were already pulled open as I viewed my train consist. I called Control feeling extremely nervous, (Operator ??? to Control. Very loud explosion. Lots of smoke. Lost my door relay before my train was berthed. People are running and screaming in fear. I'm going to check and advise.

Please standby." I didn't wait for Control to respond to me. I didn't want to waste any time. People were screaming and yelling in fear. Some saying, "IT'S A BOMB. OMG! IT'S A BOMB! I admit, I was terrified as I exited my motor cab and walked toward a huge cloud of smoke. Several riders, who rode in my head car with me, followed me as I walked to the rear of my consist. Riders ran passed me as I walked slowly thinking I might see dead bodies and my train destroyed. As I walked carefully I was praying there wasn't another explosion.

Control called me for an update. "Control I'm almost to the rear of my consist. Standby." Control called me quickly. I suppose they were very nervous as well. When I got to the 5th car of 8, 3 people were walking towards me calmly out of the smoke. They were of different nationalities. They explained what happened. All 3 said the same thing. There was a guy standing between rail cars who had a very large firework. He lit it and drop it under the train. As the 2nd person finished talking to me, the smoke started clearing. There was no fire. There was no destruction to the train. However, there was a smell of something burning. I didn't see anything burning. I called Control and gave my update. After we talked I could hear the relief in the Controllers voice. My train was practically empty now as I proceeded to Roosevelt. Control sent CTA Maintainers to check the tracks. The burning smell was the 3rd rail. It was scorched and needed to be replaced. I was so relieved it wasn't a bomb. I thanked the 3 witnesses that came forward. This delay wasn't too long, but it should have never happened. This was a very ignorant and negligent thing to do.

Speaking of ignorant and negligence, this is what a manager said to me when I was assigned my very first student train operator. I tried to decline a student, but I was encouraged to take him because I just completed training with everything fresh in my mind. I was assigned a student after being a qualified train operator for 3 weeks. They were asking me questions I couldn't even answer. We started at 95th, but never made it back to 95th. At Howard I asked a manager the question my student asked me and the manager was very upset I was given a student. They took the student to the CTA Instructors Office at Howard, and I was told do not ever take a student until you've acquired significant experience. I felt so small. I took heed though. I never had another student until many years later.

Speaking of student operators. There was a situation that took place with a student operator and a regular operator. If my memory is correct, they were at Cermak China Town northbound with a red over red signal. If you ride the CTA you will hear an announcement saying you're standing for signal clearance. The operator and their student were given instructions on how to proceed. Well, the student was operating. The student hit the wrong lever on the signal which changed the switch points. Instead of going into the subway to Roosevelt, they went over the top towards the Chicago Loop. The student was not charged with the safety violation. The regular operator was charged. The regular operator had to go through retraining. I remember when I had to go through retraining. It's almost embarrassing to a certain degree, but on the hand, it was also looked at as a vacation. Every CTA person didn't share this view. I certainly didn't. I had a reputation for being an outstanding operator. I hated doing platform at Howard. A Platform person are the people who are assigned to check the trains at Howard when Red Line trains arrive on the northbound platform. I enjoyed operating my train and I believed being a Platform person because of retraining was an insult. I enjoyed my job so much I created slogans. I had many slogans I would say to my coworkers. Some loved them and others, well… they didn't care much for them. "Happy CTA." "Let's have fun out there." "Let's all provide our customers with excellent service." I was praised by CTA Instructors for years, but that all came crashing down in a small short period of time.

I had a clear record for 13 years with no safety violations. The day before I was scheduled to fly to Trinidad I received my first CTA safety violation. I was standing at a red over red signal at Addison on the Purple Line. I was calling the Towerman on short range to give me the route. After standing for several minutes I called Control. Control started calling the Towerman as I waited for a route. I was anxious to get home so I could start packing for Trinidad. I neglected my own instructions that I taught student operators. I taught them to always watch your switch points and see exactly where you are going before you move your train. I was so frustrated I neglected the things I knew were diligent to do. As soon as the track trip went down I moved my train. I didn't look at anything as I talked to myself saying, "I'm so tired of lazy Towerman. All you got to do is push a button and you can't do that quick enough. Plus you get paid more than me…. I went on and on until my train crossed over from track 4 to track 3. I've never seen the video. I could only imagine how the look on my face changed from frustration to utter shock. My mind raced looking for options to get out of this situation. There was no way out. There was no way to get back to track 4. Control called me asking about my location. I was hesitant to respond. Control called me again. I responded, "Operator 514 northbound approaching Sheridan on track 3." Control asked me to repeat, but it was a different Controller. Then another Controller asked me my location. Well, at this point I was not going home to pack any time soon. Many of my coworkers said I did this on purpose, but I didn't. I messed up. I honestly messed up. Months later I got another safety and then another safety. I had 3 safety violations in less than 12 months. I was on the verge of being fired. Any more safety violations and it was over for me. I would no longer work at the CTA. With each safety violation I was forced to be a Platform person and could not operate a CTA train. A regular assigned Platform person could operate a train if needed. Not me. Not anyone with a safety violation. This is why I was on the platform when the young was shot at Howard. I'll never forget when a certain CTA Instructor said this to me, "Mr. Boston, you have fallen from grace." I was no longer a confident operator. Now I was overly cautious. I took my time in every situation. I couldn't have another safety for a year. Well, I made it. I made it and those safeties fell off. It was a tough time for me. I was going through a divorce and Covid protocols were in effect. During this season I wasn't taking many students. I was very selective. If you were new, nope. If you were in retraining, sure. If you were doing a refresher, sure.

At the very beginning of my day at Howard, as soon as I walked through the door, "Marcus, you got a student." I replied, "I'm not taking students." As I walked over to clock in and sign in. Someone else said, "Marcus, did you hear? You have a student." I replied stronger, "I'm not taking students!" I never looked to see who the student was because on this day I just didn't care. I filled my water bottle then went to my locker to put something inside. I returned to the break room, "Marcus you got a student." "I said I'm not taking students!" I'm sitting at the round table when the student walks over to me saying, "I'm your student for today." I didn't look up to see who it was because today was not the day, "I'm not taking students!" The student responds "Well, I'm a manager and you need to stand down..." I cut him off, "That's not how this works! I SAID I'M NOT TAKING STUDENTS!!!" Coworkers started calling my name as if this was going to calm me down. The student manager thought he had some form of authority over me. He kept talking and my coworkers were talking until I yelled, "I'M NOT TAKING STUDENT! THAT'S NOT HOW THIS WORKS! I DON'T CARE YOU'RE A MANAGER! YOU'RE A STUDENT RIGHT NOW! YOU CAN'T MAKE ME DO ANYTHING! I SAID I'M NOT TAKING STUDENTS!" Now I was pissed off. The student manager went into the Clerk's office as if someone was going to change my mind. My coworkers kept trying to get me to calm down, but I couldn't. I grabbed my backpack and headed to train early. After talking with my supervisor I went to Dunkin' to get us both some coffee. This situation pissed me off, but coffee is always a pleasure. My day cheered up as I took my deadhead to Linden. I had no interest in students who never operated a train during my probation period.

I remember when a CTA Instructor practically begged me to take a certain student. This was before I had my 3 safety violations. Let me give you a backstory before I continue with this student. My other 2 safeties were absolutely crazy by the way. During my season of hating Spotters I made enemies among them. I called them out on purpose. This one Spotter used to get on my train at Chicago & Franklin, and exited at Clark & Lake. One day when he exited he said, “Have a good day.” There was a woman standing near my motor cab window; too close if you ask me. I responded to him so I could kill 2 birds with one stone, “You too Spotter.” His face twisted as the woman started laughing. I kept a straight face. The next day this same Spotter who used to wear a suit and tie every day. On this day he still had on a suit and tie, but he chose to wear a baseball cap which he had on backwards. In addition, he's playing music on his phone. As he boarded on Chicago & Franklin he utters, "Sup." I started saying to myself, "Oh so now he's hood?" As I chuckled to myself. When he exited at Clark & Lake his music was still playing. There was another woman standing near my motor cab similar to the other woman the previous day. I purposely spoke these words in a somewhat loud voice so he could hear me over his music, "Since when they let Spotters play music and break CTA rules?" The woman's reaction said it all. She put a hand over her face. Why would a regular rider do this? After this day I never seen that man again. He rode my train for months and now he was a ghost.

Like I said, I made enemies of Spotters. I was never disrespectful, but I suppose anything I said would have been considered disrespect. My main saying was "Good job Spotter." Or "Keep up the great work Spotter." I really hated these people. I deemed them "CTA Snitches." I guess these Spotters told other Spotters until one day at State & Lake I noticed a very suspicious person. He stance was odd and he kept shades on. From the first day I saw him, he continued being at State & Lake daily. He had a backpack that was unusual too. I never said anything to this man. Everything about him was off to me. At State & Lake there is a CTA Sand Box which is just near the berthing marker for us to stop our train. Sand is used for many things such as slippery platforms and more. Every day this man's backpack was on top of the Sand Box and he would be standing in different places. See the picture. Depending on where he was located depended on if I stopped completely on the yellow or if I allowed my train to drift several feet away from the yellow tile. I never liked anyone standing near my head outside of the train window. On crowded platforms I had to ask people to give me some room. One day this guy was leaning on the railing with his right elbow on the Sand Box with his shades on. I stared at him as his body and head was perfectly lined with me on the yellow tile. My eyes looked at his backpack. I looked closer. I looked even closer. I couldn't believe my eyes. I said vocally feeling

baffled, "ARE YOU RECORDING ME?" His body language immediately shifted as I looked at him and then back at his backpack. I closed my doors and proceeded. I never seen him again. I knew I wasn't crazy, but my perception was off. Here's why I say this. There was a CTA manager that I laughed with and joked with on many occasions. I was always happy to see this manager because they were the coolest. They did there job with a smile. So I thought. One day I saw this CTA manager at Clark & Lake as I was berthing my train. I was about 50 feet from the yellow berthing marker. My eyes lit up and I placed my head outside of my window smiling. This managers face was so stern I wondered if I did something to offend them. There was no smile. No wave. No walk to my window for a quick laugh or two. These things were normal. Now I'm experiencing something that wasn't normal. Clark & Lake was full of riders so I stood a little longer as they exited and boarded my train. The entire time I looked at the manager who didn't look at me again. I started looking around and the people standing near my train all had that same stern look. I looked at each of them in the face. I had no fear or intimating factor with all I experienced at CTA at this point, however, I wasn't going to do something stupid like chasing someone who robbed somebody. I used to say to my coworkers, "I'm going home to my family. I will not die a hero at CTA." I closed the doors and looked at the manager as I pulled off. No smile. No reaction. I arrived at State & Lake still thinking of the manager. I arrived at Washington & Wabash with this manager still on my mind. Then it dawned on me. The manager was telling these people were not Spotters. They were upper level managers. I never said anything ever again. I didn't look at them anymore. I changed my entire attitude, but I believe it was too late for this. Like I was saying, my last 2 safety violations were crazy. I was given a putout from the yard. Meaning a CTA Switchman brings me a train for service. I was already late so I boarded the train and did a "Load and Go." As I pulled off I heard a sound that was very unusual. Because I was late I took a look at it at South Boulevard station. One of the springs was stretched. I secured it and proceeded. I didn't think nothing of it. The operator who received my train checked it and called the stretched spring in. Long story short I was blamed for the stretched spring. I tried to fight it, but lost. CTA Cameras weren't working, so they told me, at the time of my incident. I was given a safety, but the Switchman who brought me the train wasn't given a safety. I knew that train came out of the yard like that. The spring was stretched in the yard by a Switchman. The more I thought about it the more I believed it was a setup.

The 3rd safety was given to be because I didn't call in what I witnessed until later. I thought I saw a dead body and I didn't want to stop to see it, or smell it. I called it in later, but it turns out the person was alive and got up running away from CTA property. I was given a safety. It wasn't a safety violation. It was a procedure issue. A CTA Instructor had a real heart to heart with me. This Instructor was very bold with me. "Marcus you're not yourself. I don't know what's going on in your personal life, but you need shake it off and leave that at home. They really want to fire you. You need to focus and do your job. Forget about how you feel. Just do your job. Those last 2 safety violations…, you shouldn't have those. You should not be in this position. If you just did your job. If you called in the person on the right of way, no safety. If you checked your train before you moved it, no safety. Do your job. Forget about delays. Do your job. This is about your money now. If they riders are late, let them be late. Do your job." This talk woke me up. He's words sobered me entirely. My marriage was horrible and it did affect me. I was operating and thinking about home. When the other CTA Instructor said I fell from grace it was simply the truth. I no longer had a respected reputation with many CTA individuals. Backstory over. Let's get back to the student operator.

I took this student during the time when I was praised and respected as a good train operator. I had several commendations by the way. Anyway, this student did not qualify several times and I had no interest in having them. I heard the Instructor out and took the student. This day was just as stressful as St. Patrick's day. The student had a negative attitude and I did my best to persuade them to change how they viewed operating a train. I corrected their vocabulary often throughout the day. What I discovered about this operator is that they could operate the train decently. They could operator the train doors decently. Their problem was putting it all together. I literally had to say,

"Open the doors. Close the doors. Walk back over and move the train." For some reason it just didn't register. "Slow down. What does the signal convey? What is the correct route? We were more than 5 minutes late and I didn't take over the train. I was stressed to the point I didn't even want to operate. Control knew who I had as a student and didn't bother me. Our delay didn't mess up the entire railroad, but it messed with my frame of mind. When this day ended I couldn't wait to get home and take a hot shower. When I got off of work there was a letter for me in the clerk window saying I would have that same student tomorrow. Dang. Then I had them another day. Dang. When I was done with this student they were a much better operator. They answered my questions with ease now. I didn't have to dictate their train operations anymore. However, this student's biggest problem was their focus. They could not operate at all without staying focus. As for me I could look at rainbows. I could look at sunsets and ride with my head outside the window to get some fresh air. This student couldn't function if their focus was broken. Well, the day this student qualified had me hopeful. I kept reminding them to make sure to watch their routes at all towers. All went well until they were at Belmont northbound. The Towerman was instructed to give them the wrong route on purpose. This is done to make sure we are paying attention. Although we may have a clear route, the question is, is it the correct route? I've been given an incorrect route and would make the following announcement, "Attention Riders. We are standing waiting for the correct route from the Towerman. I do apologize for the inconvenience. We should be moving shortly." My student took the wrong route and failed the qualification. They were given a job in a different department. I felt as if my hard work with them was for nothing. At least they still had a job, but this was so sad to me. However, operating a train isn't for everyone, but this was still sad to me. There were other things on our job that caused me to be sad.

The saddest thing I believe are the people who decide to jump in front of a train to end their life. I'm so fortunate and grateful to God this never happened to me. It could have on one occasion. I stopped my train about 10 feet from this person who was already laying on the tracks at Berwyn station. I'm very glad I saw them. They were taken to a hospital alive and it was discovered they were drunk with no injuries. I've had people play as if they were going to jump in front of my train and this scared me. I started making announcements after I berthed my train in the station. "To the people playing like you're going to jump in front of my train you are not funny. Please stop it." Sometimes after I opened the doors I would take a minute to collect myself before I closed the doors to proceed to the next station. It was never funny to me. I had many coworkers who experienced "a collision of a CTA vehicle with a person." These operators needed professional counseling and needed to be medicated to help them with the trauma. Some had nightmares of the people who jumped. During my early years at the CTA, I found myself being the train that was right behind a train of such incidents. The thing that made my situation worse was the fact that I was a trapped train. A trapped train is a train that cannot be moved forward or against traffic. Against traffic means change ends and return to the previous station. When I say my riders were furious, they were furious and let me have it verbally. I took it on the chin. When I wasn't a trapped train, at least they could leave the station to catch a bus, a cab, or call a ride. After I made my manual announcement my train was empty. I would change my signs into "Out Of Service" and turn the interior lights off. I had to stay with my train. Many times I was hungry because I didn't get my lunch. Or thirsty. This is when I learned to keep water and snacks in my work bag for the just in case scenarios. I was no longer hungry or thirsty as I sat on my empty train.

My coworkers who experienced someone jumping in front of their train were off of work for almost a year or more. I asked many of them this question: What was that experience like? After receiving the same answer from them all I stopped asking. They all said this in their own way. "Well, as soon as I entered the station and applied my brakes, they came out of nowhere and jumped in front of my train. They jumped and looked me in my face as my train hit them and knocked them down to the tracks. Then I didn't see them anymore as they went under my train. It happened so fast. I have nightmares of their face looking at me. Their eyes. I can't get their eyes out of my mind." When they talked about this, each of them had similar expressions. My heart went out to them. Many of them were married with children. This was traumatic and affected their family members as well. If you're suicidal please get some help and don't jump in front of a train. The saddest one of all to me was the lady at 63rd Street station. She was holding her baby. She asked someone to hold her baby for a moment. The person agreed to hold the baby not knowing what the mother was about to do. After giving her baby to the stranger she jumped in front of the train. Can you imagine how this person felt holding her baby? The train operator and the person holding the baby were both traumatized. If you're thinking of committing suicide please get some help. Don't jump in front of a train. The Chicago Fire Department is called in the aftermath. They are the ones who do the cleanup. They gather what remains of the person who jumped. The train and the tracks are thoroughly searched and cleansed. They are very careful nothing remains of this sad circumstance. This is why it takes a very long time for train service to be restored. CTA Bus shuttle service is implemented and there's a very high probability this will be on the news. I remember the night when I was a trapped train southbound at Lake Street. I made a manual announcement, "Attention CTA Riders. This train is now out of service do to a medical emergency on the train ahead of us. I do apologize for the inconvenience. Bus Shuttle service will be provided upstairs at street level or you can take a train on the Chicago Loop elevated tracks upstairs to get to your destination. Once again I apologize for your inconvenience." I could clearly hear people cursing me out as they exited the train. My window was open and many of them shouted at me before they left the station. Then someone hit one of the emergency buttons on my train. I responded, "Can I help you?" "What do you mean they are having a medical emergency? Why can't they remove that person off the train and the train keeps going. I don't understand how the fuck you CTA people do shit…" As they talked to me I switched from talking to this person to talking over the entire train intercom system. "Attention riders. Someone jumped in front of the train ahead of us and they are underneath the train. The Fire Department has been called to remove this person's body from under the train. I'm sorry medical emergency wasn't clear enough. It will take them at least an hour. Please find other ways to get to your destination. I'm very sorry for your inconvenience." After I made this announcement everyone left without saying a word to me. One person came back to say, "I can't believe someone jumped in front of the train. That poor operator. Have a good night CTA." They walked off before I could say a word. Once again I was a trapped train, but I had water and snacks. I hated when our riders were inconvenienced. Moreover, I hated when people committed suicide by train. If you're thinking of jumping in front of a train, CTA has provided information on every platform, station, and Terminal. Please call the national SUICIDE PREVENTION LIFELINE at 1-800-273-8255 or go to this website: www.suicidepreventionlifeline.org. It's free and confidential. Please don't kill yourself. As I write this book a friend of mine contacted me saying they were in a hospital. They tried to commit suicide. I cried as they shared their story. I understand we all can experience life in very traumatic, painful, and horrible ways. Bad things happen. Sometimes they keep happening and it seems like it will never end. However, it will end if we keep living and working on making our lives better. Keep striving for better. Don't give up. Please don't give up. I'm sure you're exhausted. I understand. I've had suicidal thoughts before when I was in a very dark place. Sometimes it seems like no one cares and that no one loves you. I care about your life and I don't even know you. My heart hurts when I hear about bad things happening to strangers, and I pray for them. Just keep pressing your way until your change happens. I did and you can too.

I remember the day when I saw these signs at Howard Terminal. I pointed these signs out to my coworkers. Most of them didn't notice these signs as of yet. This was an amazing idea and I'm glad it was implemented. Once again please get help if you're having suicidal thoughts. The next chapter I will talk about the good times I've experienced at the CTA. I celebrate having great memories and I'm very happy to write them in this book.

The Good Times

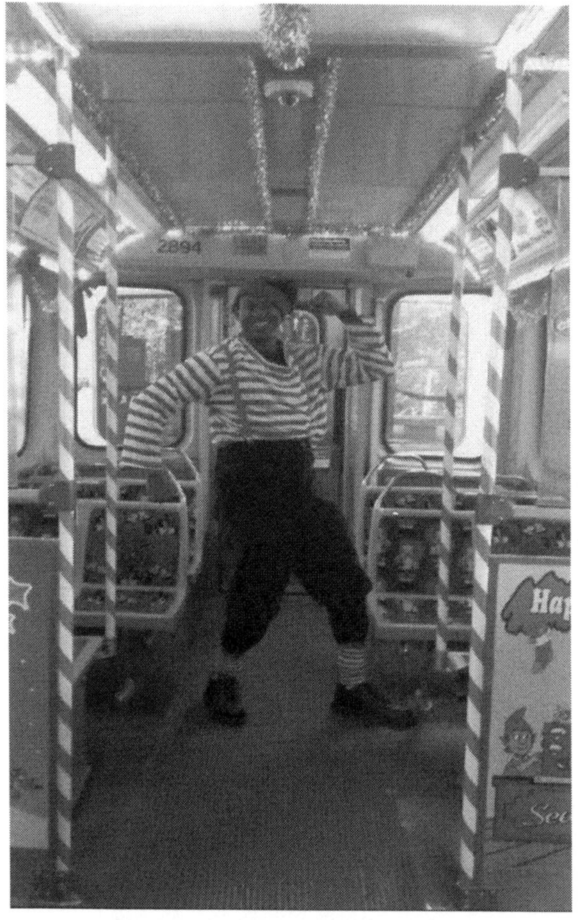

CTA ELF WORKSHOP TRAIN 2016

I enjoyed being out of 95th Terminal. This break room was the loudest out of every terminal before they built the new 95th Terminal. The break room was a place to recuperate and unwind after having a stressful trip or a stressful first half of our day. Some of us took naps, some watched movies, some played dominos, and some played cards. When I started out I used to read my bible and kept to myself. As I got to know my coworkers I opened up and started having fun. One evening at work someone brought their PlayStation 2 console to work and I was challenged to a game of Madden. I was kind enough to decline, but they kept insisting. The fellas were instigating us to play. This was the version of Madden that had the truck stick and I had a very good winning record online. We had a really good game going on. It was very competitive and we ended the game tied. I had to get back to work. We never did play again, but I gained his respect and he gained mine as well.

I appreciated the break room. We watched the Super Bowl, World Series, and many other sporting events. On those bad CTA days, even though we never called it counseling, we were there to listen, comfort, and be each other's peace on those rough days. On those days with bad major delays, many times, the television was off. We either talked about what happened, or sometimes we had nothing at all to say; especially when I was out of Howard. Howard break room became a place of therapy for me. I truly love many of my coworkers. I miss them very much.

As I became more comfortable operating the train, I started having fun with my riders. Most of the things I'm about to share happened on the old trains with "no cameras" or "train black boxes" recording everything we do as we operate the train. These things I'm about to write about I would never do on the 5000 series trains with all of the CTA cameras.

One night I was operating the train on Halloween. As my train was entering the State Street Subway I turned off the interior lights and started laughing on the intercom as if I was the killer in a horror movie. Many of the ladies screamed while the men laughed. I only had the lights off about 5 seconds. I did this a few times that night and some riders thanked me for the laughs they shared with their squad. I had a lot of fun watching the different riders in full costumes getting on and off my train. My all-time favorite Halloween memory was when I stopped at Granville. I was smiling so big when I saw this couple board my train and I told them, "Welcome Aboard." They both smiled at me. I was so happy seeing them dressed as Super Mario and the Princess.

I was instantly inspired to make an announcement as I closed the doors and proceeded to Thorndale southbound. I grabbed the handset and began to say without rehearsing, "Attention CTA riders. It's with great honor that I inform you that we have a legend aboard this train in the head car. He started out in the arcades with Donkey Kong. He's had several hit video games on Nintendo, Super Nintendo, and so on through the years. Can you please give a big round of applause for..., Super Mario!!!" I made sure to say Super Mario in a very dramatic way. Everyone began to clap their hands and I added, "And yes, he has the Princess with him. Mario finally has the Princess." The CTA riders exploded into cheers, laughter, and clapping that lasted for several minutes. I was very happy so many people got what I was saying. When Super Mario and the Princess exited my train many station stops later, they both approached my train window. He sincerely said, "We both really appreciate what you said about us. This made our night. Thank you so much." I replied, "You are very welcome and thanks for riding the CTA." They both laughed as I smiled at them. They walked off slowly with his arm around the Princess who was genuinely his princess. This was a fun night and the thing I also remember is that I didn't have any delays or train malfunctions that night. It was a very good night on the Red Line.

Another good night was when the Chicago Black Hawks won the Stanley Cup. Once again I was on the intercom saying things to get my riders cheering. "Let's Go Black Hawks!!!" On this night my train was filled to capacity. I was giving high fives to my riders as they slowly boarded my train and when they exited. I loved when any Chicago team were the champions. I enjoyed having a train full of happy riders. Happy CTA riders were always the best riders. I remember one time when I blew a station. Blowing a station is when you completely passed it and didn't stop. I didn't try to cover it up or give fake information. I owned it. Wait Marcus. Isn't this a safety violation? Yes it is a safety, but here's what happened. The CTA supervisor at Howard gave me a double express run. Howard to Davis. Davis to Central. I was new to the Purple Line and I didn't like how my supervisor talked to me. When I went Davis to Central I forgot to stop. There were no slow zones on the Purple Line at this time. I made an announcement apologizing to the riders. I also informed them as soon as I arrived at Linden, I would change ends and go right back out. I asked them to stay abound and not exit. When I arrived at Linden the riders were smiling at me and encouraging me. When I entered the train on the opposite end these riders were nice and encouraging too. When they exited at Central they told me to have a great day and don't let CTA stress me out. When I said I owned it, I didn't own it to CTA. I didn't tell on myself. Since no one on the train called CTA I didn't receive any discipline. Happy riders don't snitch when you mess up, happy riders have your back, and happy riders desire to see CTA train operators happy. This situation was a "happy mess up."

I'm not going to say all train operators mess up, but there is a high probability they will mess up. We are human and humans are imperfect. I wasn't going to share my happy mess ups. I have several. Fortunately for me there were no cameras when I experienced my happy mess ups. Here's the truth about cameras and the CTA. When I started in 2006, cameras were only in the areas where high crime took place. Cameras were from North & Clybourn to 95th Terminal on the Red Line. I can't speak for the other train lines. There were no cameras from Fullerton to Howard Terminal. My first 7 years at the CTA were on the Red Line. When I started CTA there was not much crime taking place from Fullerton to Howard. As crime began happening where there were no cameras CTA added cameras. Now the entire CTA has cameras. I'm glad my mess ups weren't tragic. I'm glad no one got hurt. I'm about to share a big mess up I had that I had no idea I was doing.

When the new Howard Terminal was under construction, I heard the following on short range, "You're cut operator." I replied, "10-4." My 8 car train was now a 4 cars. My route was already in. I prepared my train for service without checking it. "Load & Go." Load & Go has got many operators in trouble. You already read about me getting a safety because I didn't check my train before I proceeded. I'll share one such operator story. This operator left Howard with Load & Go. Little did they know they were given a train that had several mechanical problems the day before. This train had multiple doors that didn't work on several rail cars and other issues. This operator train broke down and when they called in their issues, they were treated shamefully over the radio. I was the immediate train follower. By the time they arrived at 95th I was late right along with them. They were written up because they didn't check their train for service. We operators load and go as a convenience to the riders and the CTA. This experienced operator was crushed and this operator made the CTA pay for writing them up. I was their immediate train follower until we picked new schedules. Once they were back operating their train, CTA paid the price. Every day this experienced operator checked their train for service. They didn't care it was the morning rush hour. They didn't care about the delays already in place. This operator checked their train for service and guess what? There was absolutely nothing any CTA person could do about it. This was standard CTA policy. This operator who was a superb operator. They came to work, they had one of the better job attitudes, they had good job character, and they treated everyone with good common courtesy. I paid the price too because I was the train behind them. As long as we were on time I was good. It was when we experienced delays that my day became longer. I benefited with overtime slips, lol. This operator checked their train every day and ignored the comments on the radio. Honestly, I didn't blame them. Once I had 3 safeties I checked my train and didn't load & go anymore. This operator became hated by some and more respected by operators like myself. I had no intention of adding this story. Now let's get back to my mess ups.

Like I was saying I thought I had a 4 car train. I did not check my train. I did a load & go. I was so happy I had a train full of happy riders. I stopped at Jarvis, Morse, Granville, Thorndale, and Bryn Mawr at the 4 car marker. Loyola southbound marker is for all train consists. When I arrived at Bryn Mawr I stopped at the 4 car marker. A rider hit the emergency button and said, "Hello… Ummm, we don't have a platform to get off the train." My heart sunk immediately. I stood up and leaned far outside of my window to see my entire train consist entirely. I had 8 cars! I ran over and closed the doors. I eased up to the 8 car marker and popped the doors open without sticking my head outside. My heart was racing! I started thinking of worse case scenarios! What if someone stepped off the train and is now at track level? I was not about to call myself in. Nope. Not happening. There were no cameras on the trains or platforms at this time on the north side of Chicago. I was terrified I would get that call from Control saying, “Did anything unusual happen with your train?” Anytime Control calls us saying this there was a high possibility someone called in something that occurred. If you knew you did something fear gripped your heart. Once cameras were everywhere no one got away with anything. There were people who thought they got away with something, but this happened. While managers were checking video on other operators who were being investigated of doing something wrong, they found other operators guilty of certain things. Things they thought they got away with. Things that got some of them fired like this one operator who was found on video watching Netflix as they operated their train. I thought about my life as I operated my train. I didn't do anything that could cause me to end up dying. I wanted to go home to my family. It was all about my safety first. I wasn't going to do anything that would hurt me. I wanted to keep us all safe and we all go home to our families. I was overjoyed no one was hurt when I thought I had 4 rail cars. This could have been very tragic. This shook me to my core and this never happened again. Because of this incident, I always went to the 8th car maker on my first trip if I didn't check my train. Happy riders make all the difference as far as I'm concerned. They definitely made my day much easier.

Another happy mess up I had was when I had a student. This student did great until were arriving at Jarvis. All we had to do was stop at Jarvis and go to Howard. Then we go home. We were approaching Jarvis northbound at 15 mph with a red over red signal just passed Jarvis. The signal cleared which gave us the ability to go 25 mph. When they speeded up I didn't see a problem. We can stop at the 8 car mark as long as the brakes are applied about one third to half way in the station. When I saw they didn't apply the brakes, I told them to brake the train. They didn't put the train in brake. I said it again more strongly and they didn't brake the train. I jumped over and applied the emergency brake but I was too late. The first car of our train was outside of the station. They snapped out of whatever it was that had their mind and focus off. I didn't have time to talk. I grabbed my key, opened the motor cab door, cut out the doors in the head car, and ran back into my motor cab to open my doors. Fortunately for me no one in my head car was getting off my train. Once everyone exited my train I closed the doors and took over the train while my student was saying how sorry they were as I moved the train to Howard. I told them to get focused. I gave them control over the train then went to cut the doors back in. We arrived at Howard and went home. I was hoping what happened was not found on video as managers investigated other operators. Once again happy riders didn't call CTA about what happened. They were smiling when I cut out the doors and when I cut the doors back in they were smiling. I could have been had my first safety on my record. Thank God for happy riders.

Another happy moment for me was meeting Mayor Rahm Emanuel at Howard Terminal. Our CTA President and Mayor Emanuel came to Howard. One of my coworkers took this pic of me when I had the honor of shaking his hand. This was really cool.

The day President Obama came to Chicago, his motorcade drove adjacent to my train on the Purple Line when I was headed to South Blvd. A CTA manager was also in my motor cab when this happened. I blew my train horn and waved at him. I moved over and let the manager operate so he could wave at the motorcade too. We laughed so much on our way to Linden.

Early in my CTA career I wasn't always on the train. Before I had to choose, (freeze) a specific position, I was a Combine Rail Operator. I was on the CTA Extra Board. I didn't have a set schedule on a weekly basis. I might be on the train or I could be a Customer Assistant, Flag Man, or Switchmen. The one thing I loved was being an "Information Specialist" or doing "Crowd Control." The first time I was an Information Specialist was too funny for me because I was still new to Chicago. I didn't know directions to popular places. I had a CTA map with me and learned to ask them the address. If I couldn't find it on the map I called 1-888-Your-CTA for directions. LMBO!!! The looks on the

CTA customers faces were priceless and their comments I've never forgotten. "How come you don't know where this is and you work for the CTA?" "Don't y'all have an address class?" I told them all the truth. "I'm from Florida, I moved to Chicago, and started working here. There was no address class. I don't know this city yet. I'll call for directions." I said this so many times in various ways. The visitors to Chicago had more understanding than the Chicago natives. However, I've taken plenty of pictures with visitors from out of town. If you have a picture with me please post it and tag me in the photo, or dm it to me. The picture I remember the most were these two Asian men who wanted to take a picture with me. I was working Customer Assistant at Polk subway station. I declined this picture, but they took a moment and gave me a business card. After I read this business card I said yes. I took a picture with them and one of them says, "If you ever want a job in Japan give me a call." I was blown away. I still have this business card today. Wait..., maybe not. I know I had it prior to moving to Tampa.

The other picture I remember clearly is the cover of this book. I was leaving Clark & Lake. I looked down and saw this man with a camera. I quickly stuck my head outside of the window and gave him a thumbs up. I laughed so hard to myself because I loved when tourist took pics. I stuck my head outside of the window many times through the years. Once again, if you have pictures of me, please contact me. The book cover picture has a nice story. One day at work a coworker says, "Hey Marcus. I think I saw a picture of you on Facebook. We're not sure if it's you or not." Honestly I do not remember how I found this picture, but I did and I remembered it clearly. I just tried to find my pic again on Facebook and couldn't find it. I wanted to name the person who took the photo. I thought I tagged myself, but this pic is not in my tagged photo folder. I am so disappointed I can't share their name.

Crowd Control was a lot of fun because it was normally at a baseball game or a popular event day when certain CTA stations will be packed with customers. Most times it was a crowd of happy riders unless we loss. One time when the Chicago White Sox loss and I was the train operator, I made this announcement, "Attention everyone. This specific train is only for Chicago White Sox fans. Only Chicago White Sox fans aboard this train. Thank you." The look on the opposing team fans was priceless as they stepped back from boarding the train. I laughed so hard and finally announced, "Just kidding. All aboard." The opposing team laughed as they stepped up to board. I always tried to make my job fun.

When Michael Jackson passed I took it hard. I didn't know I loved him so much although I've never met him. Memories of the one and only concert I attended with my oldest sister Deborah Jones quickly entered my mind. In 1984 I had great seats at Comiskey Park. I didn't need a screen to see The Jackson's. We were probably 30 rows back from the stage. What an amazing concert! When MJ passed I listened to his music while I operated my train. This happened prior to our 0 cellphone policy and this would get any CTA train operator fired these days. When I had to turn my train at Howard, I decided to play MJ over the interior and exterior speakers. Billie Jean was bumping! I played it going around the "Mainline Loop" and into the southbound station. I had to keep my train and I kept it playing while my riders boarded. This was a weekday just as the pm rush was beginning. No one called me to cut it off. Not a manager or a supervisor. It was bumping! When I left Howard I turned it off and focused on operating. Control called me at Wilson to remain standing because of a delay ahead of me. I made my manual announcement and while we stood on our delay I played more MJ. The Wilson station supervisor came out of his wooden booth smiling. He walked over to my window laughing. He said, "Man you crazy." We both laughed. I started doing some MJ dances and we laughed some more. When Control called me to proceed we gave each other a pound before I closed the doors to leave the station. This was the only day I did this. The only other time I played music on the intercom was when Christmas time came. I would play Christmas music over the intercom when I rode through the subway. I loved when riders exited my train saying thanks for the Christmas music. There was a coworker who played music on short range and this was always funny. Sometimes the songs made me dance. This coworker provoked me to play music on short range as well. We used to have so much fun as we operated our trains. We used to have full conversations on short range in delays or encouraging words during stressful days. Many times on short range we assisted each other with troubleshooting our trains. Most CTA train operators looked out for each other. There was a CTA worker who didn't care for me. One night this CTA worker was on the 87th Street station. I saw him in the distance. I was not on a train. This night I was flagging, but our workers were late arriving. Control told us to remain at 87th for another hour. In the distance I saw 2 guys circling this CTA coworker who didn't care for me. We had words a few times. It looked as if these 2 guys were going to jump him. I gathered my thoughts and made up my mind to help him. I prepared my mind to fight. I walked to him as they still circled him. It was nighttime and the 3 of them were the only people on the platform. As I drew closer I had a very stern facial expression. I strongly said now that I was 10 feet away, "Are you good over here?" He answered, "I'm good." Those guys stopped circling him and walked away. Moments later a northbound train arrived and those guys boarded it. My coworker stood there as the train departed and I walked back to where I stood waiting for the workers to arrive. My coworker and I never talked about this. As a matter of fact, we never talked again; ever. I didn't have to wonder if he would have helped me if the shoe was on the other foot. The fact he didn't say thanks said it all. I appreciate my boys in Tampa that had my back and I had theirs. 2AM. Alton - Alphonso – Marcus = 2AM. This was our posse slash crew slash squad back in the day. There were others who rocked with us, but we weren't changing our name for anyone. 2AM will be a book. I learned a valuable lesson from this incident. I shouldn't get involved or help people that wouldn't help me. I never did this again. Whenever I witnessed anything remotely close to this incident, I called Control and let them call the police. Now there are several coworkers out of Howard that I would definitely assist with these hands. Yes I love Jesus. No if, ands, or buts. There are people I love out of Howard and I know I would physically fight with/for them if they were being attacked. Howard Terminal is my family. I loved them when I worked with them and I still love them now. I wasn't ready to resign and move on from the CTA. You'll learn why I resigned in the next chapter. Over the years some amazing coworkers were assaulted on duty and this crushed our job morale. It put us on edge. We worked with our guards up. We only relaxed in our break room. We focused before going to our train. We put our game faces on. We understand what CTA says. We know what CTA wants from us. We complained for years about things on the job and most things were never changed. For example: smelly stinky trains. I hated working on trains that smelled like urine and booty. Don't blame the homeless people. The regular riders used the train as a restroom too. Number 1 and number 2. I've had to isolate many rail cars for human waste. During my talk with a CTA trauma counselor, they shared how some smells are very traumatic. There was this one man who rode the train who had maggots on him. It was one of the worst smells I've ever breathed. One night I visited a church and when I walked inside, there was that same smell. That same man was sitting in this church and no one sat anywhere near him. I don't know what his health issues were, but he rode our trains regularly. He always had a newspaper and placed it in his seat before he sat down. I called him "The Newspaper Man." I hated when he boarded my train. His stench flooded the air. People would run out of the rail cars he was in into another rail car. I hated when I had to operate a train that was completely stinky. Like most CTA employees, I started bringing my own products to clean my trains. During one schedule pick we had on the Purple Line, I got to keep the same train during my first half of work and on my second half of work. I didn't have to keep cleaning my train every trip. I only cleaned each end of the same train and I was good for the rest of the day. I know I was supposed to "trim" my rear motor cab door once I've completed my operations, but I didn't because I didn't want anyone possibly leaving human waste. CTA "wrote up" many of us for not trimming the motor cab for customer use. Meaning riders couldn't enter the rear section of the train because the door is blocking their entrance. When my train record was clean I didn't trim the motor cab. It's so disgusting to walk in smelling and seeing a pile of human waste. The CTA "Car Servers" cleaned it up many times, but in more severe cases the train was taken into the yard to be thoroughly cleaned. I know it's not CTA's fault people are leaving human waste. The thing I hated the most about people who urinated on the train are the men who purposely urinated in the vents. So disgusting! I'm operating my train and when I open the doors the vent is blowing straight up on me with the smell of urine. I started turning off the air comfort and spraying things into the vent to kill the smell. After spraying I waited several stations and then turned the air comfort back on. It worked. No more urine smell. Men stop urinating in the vents! Then you have the crazy riders, male and female, who stand in-between the train urinating while the train is moving. And, of course, the many people who leave human waste on the platforms and stations. Many people do this to upset us who work at the CTA. They do it by leaving it in places where we cannot miss it so they can upset us. Many times when stopping my train in a station there was human waste exactly where I was supposed to stop. I called it in so a janitor could be sent to clean it up. I hated talking about this, but my writing flowed this way. I only wanted to talk about the good times. So on that note I'm going to end this chapter talking about my most joyous occasion at the CTA: being an elf during Christmas

When I first saw the CTA Christmas train I fell in love with it. It didn't take long before I desired to be an elf and ride with Santa. After my 4th year at the CTA, I started asking different people how do I be an elf? I kept asking but I got nowhere. As the years went by I still desired to be an elf, but I was never given the correct information. In 2016 when I walked into the Howard Terminal break room, it was full of CTA Holiday Train staff. As I walked to clock in I saw a man who was in an elf uniform. I was not happy seeing him with all the things I was told through the years. I had never seen a man as an elf although I wanted to be one. When I saw him I vocally said, "I wanted to be an elf. Since when y'all started taking men?" I was answered by an amazing person who was in charge. She asked my name and asked, "Mr. Boston, do you really want to be an elf?" "Yes." I confidently answered. "Ok. Give me your Terminal information and phone number." After I gave her my information she responds, "Mr. Boston, you are now an elf.

Welcome aboard." "For real? Oh my God! Thank you." I uttered with total joy.

She explained CTA had two trains this year and needed more elves. The Christmas Train / Holiday Train with Santa and the new "Elf Workshop Train" without Santa. The Elf Workshop Train was also known as the "Chaser Train" because it's following the train with Santa, trying to catch his train. I thought this was so cool. I was overjoyed to be an elf even though I wasn't going to ride with Santa. My only disappointment was because the Elf Workshop Train was only on the weekends. The Holiday Train was scheduled throughout the week and the weekend.

When I learned who were the elves on the Elf Workshop Train, we started having jokes about being a weekend elf. "I want to be a full time elf." "Well, I guess being a part time elf is better than no elf." "Why Santa doing us like this? We can't feed our families with this part time elf money." "We have to face it. We are not Santa's favorite elves. I guess we'll be on the island of misfit toys." Lol. We were having a laughing good time with so many different jokes. When the Holiday Train elves boarded there train I would say, "There goes those high class elves. What's wrong with us Santa, huh? What did we do Santa?" We would be laughing. It was all fun though.

I loved the entire atmosphere of Christmas. The music, the decorations, and all the happy faces. I appreciated being an elf. We were trained to be an elf. We were trained to be respectful and kind. We were trained to be in the Christmas spirit. This was easy for me. I was so happy and my elf name was "Joyful Elf." I named myself. I wasn't satisfied with the name I was given and I asked if I could change my name. When I was told yes, "Joyful Elf " was born. I had so much fun with the children and their parents.

The only times I wasn't having fun was when I helped troubleshoot the train. Elves were supposed to monitor their CTA radios at all times regardless of the Christmas festivities taking place. There were times when we had to keep an eye on certain people while staying in festive mode. Short range radio chatter was normally something of little importance. We would sometimes joke on the radio and managers were tell us to kindly stay off the radios. Sometimes short range radios had some small complications. The train operator may call to certain elves to perform troubleshooting in the rail car they were assigned in. Every once in a while, a Grinch would board the train and tried to be a blizzard of negativity to stop us from enjoying ourselves. Sometimes we had to remove individuals like this from the train. I was so happy being an elf. When we took pictures we called them, "Elfies," we took a lot of pictures. It was so much fun being Joyful Elf. I loved dancing with the children and being silly. I miss it. I really do miss it. I have many outstanding memories with the Christmas Train Staff. I was so blessed to be an elf 2016, 2017, 2018, and 2020. I did not be an elf in 2019 because I was depressed. 2019 was the year I didn't have any Christmas spirit. I tried to find it. I tried listening to Christmas music and I turned it off. I just couldn't do it. Little did I know the following year would add to my depression. 2018 was so much fun and I had the opportunity to be an elf on the train with Santa a few times. I was still the part time elf, but I was so content now. I stopped with the jokes between Holiday Train elves and Elf Workshop Train elves. It was an amazing year and I won an award for being a great elf. I'll always cherish these years as Joyful Elf. Thank you CTA.

Holidaygram
Holiday Train
1,000,000 likes

Season's Greetings
Crew

2018 CTA Holiday Train

The End Of The Line

At the beginning of 2020 I had no clue for what was coming. My church was declaring "It's My 20/20 Vision Year," but no one saw it, no one proclaimed it, and no one prophesied what 2020 really was going to be. No one was prepared. I was already in a bad situation before the lockdowns. The last good experience I had was when Chris Tucker came to The Chicago Theater in February. I bought tickets for my wife and I, and hoped to have a great time, which I did, but it didn't help my overall situation. My birthday came and I had no desire to do anything. Not even the things I loved doing. Then came the lockdown. Ugh.

I recently accessed my old Snap Chat and I found a video I made of me preparing to go to my train. I'll share a screenshot of what I found. During the Covid lockdown, CTA gave us a sign to isolate us on our train.

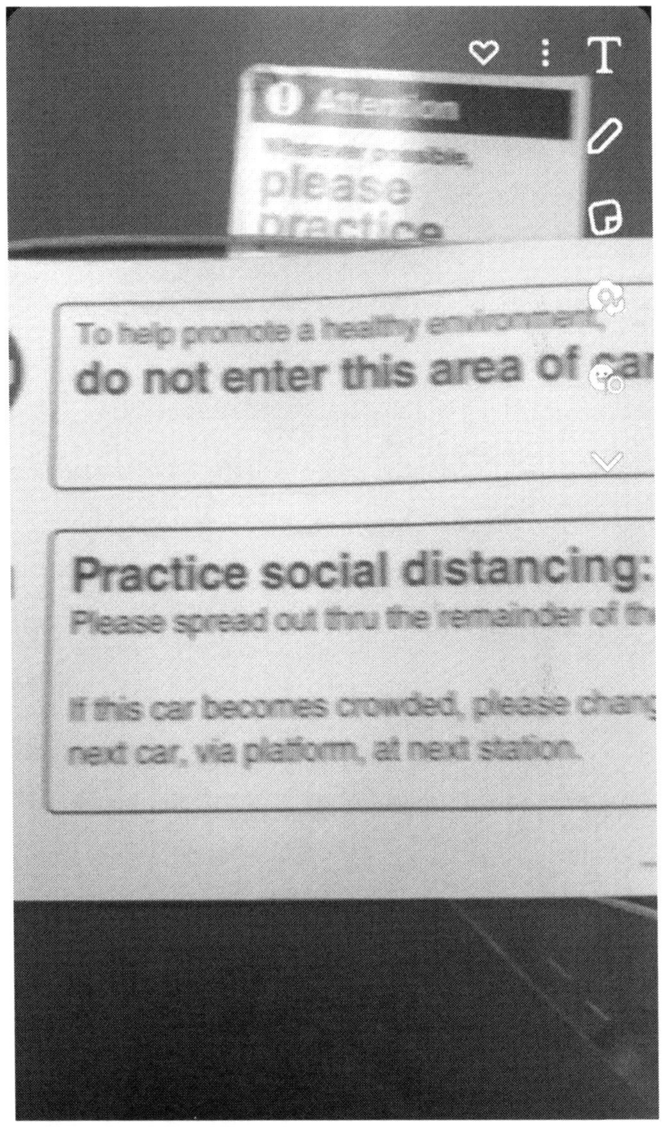

We placed this sign up so no one sat near the door of the motor cab where I operated the train. So if I needed to leave to troubleshoot, I didn't have to be within 6 feet of any rider. However, when the lockdown happened our trains were empty. I came to work every day. CTA employees who started wearing masks were told to stop wearing them because we didn't want to panic our riders. Then mask mandates happened. I didn't want to wear a mask, and I didn't until CTA threatened to suspend me. My logic was this: our trains are empty. No one was on my train so why do I need a mask? I complied although I didn't want to.

About a month or so into the lockdown I came to work on a Monday. I clocked in and signed for the bulletins. I went to my train. I'm waiting… and still waiting… The few people who rode CTA trains began to populate the platform. I called Control informing them I'm still waiting for my train. I didn't know it, but there was a quarantine taking place at Howard. There was only 1 switchman working the entire Howard yard. When I saw him on the platform I asked a few questions and he told me everything you're reading now. About 10 minutes later he brought me my train. I was not the CTA employee who hung out with my coworkers often. This wasn't on purpose. I was invited to a few things and I went to have a good time. I was busy with church events and writing books. I was the last person to learn many things taking place at CTA over the weekends. This quarantine was new to me. Covid swept through the CTA. Manpower was very low. I remember the first person who had Covid out of Howard. The seriousness of this virus was not yet released so I had no fear or caution. This case led to our first quarantine of CTA employees out of Howard. I came to work and my coworker didn't look so good. I walked over to them and put my arm around their shoulder. "You don't look so good (name). You sure this isn't Corona?" CTA employees do not have sick days. Most of us at CTA cannot afford to be off work a single day. "But y'all make blah blah blah." Half of our blah blah blah is what we take home.

Deductions are: Pension Pre-Tax, HC Trust, Medicare, Federal Tax, State Tax, Health Insurance, Dental, Social Security, Union Dues, and sometimes Special Union Dues. Doesn't sound too good now huh? But it's a living. With no sick days and "with the protocols that happen when we get sick and call off," if we can work sick, we are going to work sick. If your sickness or illness doesn't meet the "protocols" you don't get paid. Remember when I told you my doctor kept me off of work? Well, I was approved for short term disability. This paid me $200.00 a week. I was looking to move into my own place, but God told me not to do it. I lived at home with my mom. I wanted to move so I could shut the mouths of women. Well, if I would have moved out I would have lost everything. That $200.00 a week I thought I was getting; Child Support took it. I had checks totaling $13.00. I have one child. I called Child Support in Florida and they said, "Well, your child still has to eat Mr. Boston." "What about me eating? I need to eat!" Child Support didn't care. Here I was working at CTA full time, but now on short term disability and I applied for food stamps. I was approved. What could I do with $13.00? I couldn't afford to pay my mobile phone bill. It was turned off. I didn't have money saved up for various reasons. I lost so much. I'm glad I wasn't dating. I needed to get back to work and when I finally did return to CTA, I made sure I wasn't going to be off again unless I couldn't operate the train. I came to work sick. Most of us came to work sick because we couldn't afford to stay home eating soup and taking pills. Bills needed to be paid. So there I was with my arm around my sick looking coworker. They did not look good. I worked my day and I later found out they had Corona. The next day when I clocked out from work I wasn't feeling well. I told the clerk. I went home and work up in the middle of the night with a fever. I called off and hoped I didn't have Covid. This was a Friday. I had this fever all day. Saturday morning I still had a fever and my wife started calling around for Covid test centers. All of a sudden, my fever broke and I felt great. I had no other symptoms. I called the clerk and I was back to work on Monday. I had weekends off and only missed that one day of work.

Like you already know my marriage was unhealthy. The details of this marriage is in my book, “From Woman To Woman” Volume Three if you’re curious of what happened. My wife cooked meals a few times a week. What I am about to share is something I figured out later. I believe I had Covid. All of the symptoms were not yet released to the public. My wife was a very good cook, but now all of her food tasted bland. I didn’t complain because of the state of our marriage. I recall the day I ordered food from Red Lobster. I brought her lunch that day. I had my favorites and my food had no taste at all. I couldn’t taste those biscuits, my coconut shrimp, or my Cajun Chicken Pasta. I was so mad! Things with my wife got out of control and I moved out. Soon thereafter I woke up to get ready for work and my coffee had an aroma that filled the air. It smelled so good and tasted amazing. When I went to work the television was on at Howard. They shared interviews with those who had Covid and when they said, “I still can’t taste or smell.” My mouth dropped! I was so shocked and thankful that my symptoms wasn’t worse. My coworker had it pretty bad, but recovered. They didn’t need to be hospitalized. My wife didn’t get sick from me. We weren’t kissing or having sex anymore in our marriage. It was dead. No passion. No fun. It was a very sad depressing mess, but I’m glad she didn’t get sick from me. However, she did catch Covid. Someone screenshot her post on social media saying she had Covid Delta and shared it in my dm. I called up some praying people and we interceded for her. I heard she made a full recovery.

When I clocked in for work there were many train runs that said, “No Manpower.” See pic below.

811	18 red RTO	0644		no manpower	Y/N	
514	18 purple RTO	0656	44512	Boston, Marcus	Y/N	
812	18 red RTO	0658		no manpower	Y/N	
813	18 [illegible] RTO	0710		no manpower	Y/N	

There were days on the train where I didn’t see a CTA supervisor or manager. CTA offered overtime for almost every position. I didn't do it. I was still on probation and didn't want to risk getting that last safety on my day off. More and more of us were quarantined. One of our coworkers fought Covid for many months and was finally Covid free, but they later passed during rehabilitation. I was crushed. I didn't know this coworker personally. They were not out of Howard, but my heart went out to his family.

2020 was a very painful year. So many of our hearts ached at CTA. Hearts all over the world ached in like manner. I've never went to so many funerals in such a short time and I was going through a divorce. I reached the point where I couldn't go to another funeral. I was depleted emotionally. I had nothing left within to attend another homegoing. What I will say is that my Howard family helped me get through this season. We helped each other get through it. We lost some coworkers, some family members, some friends, and some friends of our families. We were there for each other. I myself started professional counseling online and I did it in the break room at Howard. My coworkers supported me. There were times I cried and released during counseling. No one cracked jokes. No one made fun of me. I was hurting and it was clearly noticeable. I started letting my hair grow and I got twists. My hair fell out because of the stress I endured. One coworker told me the truth sincerely, "Marcus, you need to cut your hair so it's all even. It doesn't look good." I wasn't angry or upset. I appreciated them. Truth is shared when someone cares enough for you. I cut my hair. I slowly improved with counseling, but then CTA comes with mandatory Covid vaccinations. I was pro vaccinations until a coworker died who was vaccinated. Then another coworker died. Maybe I was a conspiracy theorist, but I no longer wanted it and it turns out I probably would have died if I took it. My blood pressure was through the roof and I was unaware of it. 248/188. I also caught Bell's Palsy again, but this time I couldn't go to my doctor. I called but no one answered. I left messages and no one returned my calls. I prayed everyone at my doctor's office was well. I'm sure 2020 affected them negatively in some fashion. I exercised my face and started eating healthier and doing better. My blood pressure dropped down to 148/98. Then a few weeks later it was 129/90. It took my face two months to recover and I still have some right facial weakness. I still didn't desire the vaccination. CTA started firing people for not being vaccinated. I really didn't want to resign.

During my swing breaks I spent time trying to find Lysol spray, Lysol wipes, Clorox wipes, and rubbing alcohol. My swing break lasted almost 4 hours. I kept finding these items and posting them on Facebook so others could benefit. So many people thanked me. It got to the point where people looked to my page to find these items. I posted pictures and the address where those items could be found.

When I wasn't running around for those items, I wrote books during my breaks. When I started CTA in 2006 I was already working on my first book, "A Pastor's Mistake." It was published in 2007. I've worked on many books on my breaks through the years. I would sit in the back of Howard with my laptop. I wrote, "For Better Or Worse. Why Christians Get Divorced?" while I was separated. I then wrote the workbook and 4 other books before my last day at CTA. I was encouraging my coworkers to write a book while I worked there. I told my manager I was going to write a book about CTA. My manager had a look of concern. I added, "It will be a good book about the CTA." I believe this is a good book. I loved working at the CTA. It wasn't perfect. No job or company is perfect. Just think about it this way. CTA is a job that serves the public. Look at the issues Chicago has with CTA service. Is the issue CTA or is it the public? The best of Chicago rides the CTA and the worst of Chicago rides the CTA. Trains and Buses break down. It happens. That's on us. Signals, train tracks, train circuits, etc., need repairs; that's on us. People holding doors, pulling doors, fighting, selling, hustling, etc., that's the public. That's not us. That's not our fault. I asked so many people to call CTA and complain about their concerns. 1-888-Your-CTA. Most problems on CTA property are really not CTA's fault. Human waste is not CTA's fault. That's the public. Would I come back to work at CTA? Yes. I can say through my 16 years at CTA there are only a few people I had issues with. I get along with most people and I most certainly got along with most supervisors and managers. If I came back to CTA I would not be a train operator. Prior to getting my first safety I desired to be the head of the safety department. I was looking into moving up when I received my first safety. In order to move up you can't have any safeties on your record. Well, that eliminated me. At the time the position wasn't filled. I have many ideas to improve safety. Nope, I'm not writing them in here lol. If I came back I would be looking to be in the safety department, but if I still need to be vaccinated, well, that eliminates me lol.

Once I submitted my resignation letter my attitude changed. I started having more fun on my job and my happiness increased. Our trains were still empty for most of my remaining time, but there was a slight rider increase. I continued with counseling and I stopped looking for Lysol etc.. I spent my time having a good time with my coworkers. While having a good time in the Howard break room, I discovered TikTok. I wasn't on TikTok like everyone else, but once I discovered it, I loved it. My first viral video was me dancing in the Howard break room before I went to my train for my first run. When I returned for my swing break I was already viral. The numbers keep rising. I couldn't believe I had a viral video. I did another video with me coming off my train at Linden and dancing. This video went viral as well. My 2nd viral video was shared on Instagram and Facebook where it also went viral. My manager asked me to come in their office. I was kindly and respectfully asked to stopped making videos. A New York train operator wanted to challenge me on TikTok, but now that CTA was watching me closely I didn't try to do another video on my train. After my manager talked to me I received a phone call from Control.

They asked me if I was trying to get fired. I replied no, and I didn't inform them I submitted my letter of resignation. Control specifically said, "We are watching your video Mr. Boston. Upper level management have their eyes on you. You need to stop before you lose your income." After this conversation which took place in the clerk's office, I knew CTA was watching me closely. I wasn't free to make anymore videos. I stopped. I really stopped, but after a week I started making break room videos again. I still love looking at these videos today.

My last day at the CTA was April 8th, 2022. I couldn't believe it. My last trip on the Purple Line was very sad to me. I loved operating my train. I loved crossing the Chicago River and I loved seeing the Chicago Skyline. I loved CTA. The idea of being a public servant was beautiful to me. One of my highlights on this job was when my train was chosen for the CTA Red Line South Reconstruction Project. It was posted on YouTube on May 17, 2013 on the "Chicago Mayor's Office" page. I'm looking at it now and Rahm Emanuel's face is still on the profile. A camera crew boarded my train at Cermak China Town and recorded me operating my train all the way to 95th Terminal. I answered several questions about the slow zones we had at that time. I was so honored. I will never forget that day because at the time they boarded my train, a veteran CTA operated shouted on the CTA a call code for an emergency. There was a derailment on the CTA Corridor between Fullerton and Armitage.

I loved watching CTA Connections on public access in Chicago. I was proud to be in the CTA family. I'm so grateful to have been in the family and I wrote this book with all good intentions. I hope it came across in a good way. I wanted to be honest about the good and bad that happened. Many things I purposely didn't share and will never share in any book. I didn't use any names on purpose. As I bring this book to a close, I can say it's been a wonderful ride. I hate that I never moved up in the company. It would have been nice to be a supervisor or an instructor. My ultimate goal was to be the head of the CTA Safety Department. I really believed I could have made a difference. To everyone at Howard, Linden, and 95th , I love you. To the CTA Holiday Train and Elf Workshop Train crews, thank you so much for letting me be a part of the amazing festivities. To my favorite supervisors, instructors, and managers, thank you for everything you did to make me a better operator. As always "be safe" and "Thank You For Working At The CTA." To Pete's Grill, Subway, Dunkin' Donuts, Jewels, Walgreens, Buffalo Joe's, Good To Go, Da Jerk Pit, Lil Wok, Redz Belizean Restaurant, and Harold's Chicken, thanks for all the laughs while providing me with the items I wanted. I pray blessings over my CTA family and all of these businesses.

My last train ride from Linden to Howard didn't seem real. I did something I would never do. I recorded my last train consist at Linden prior to departing for Howard. "Linden Resort," as I called it, was a place of great conversations and laughs. I have tons of great memories at Linden. As I departed Linden for the last time I really felt it. My train was almost empty. When I arrived at Howard I was reminded of the foolishness that takes place. I had a 6 car train and someone pulled a door open. I still had 2 cars outside of Howard. A CTA Car Servicer reset my door and I berthed my train. I opened the doors for the last time. When I closed them I felt it.

As I made my way to Howard break room a sadness hit me. I really didn't want to resign. I didn't want to go. I entered Howard break room and looked around for a moment. My manager called me into their office. It was time to fill out the paperwork. I informed them I wasn't doing the 2nd half of my day. This was it. I had to surrender my keys, my cards, and my equipment. I had to clean out my locker and give up my locker key. It didn't take 10 minutes. I sat there in disbelief. I was no longer an employee at the Chicago Transit Authority. My amazing Howard family had a card for me. I took lots of pictures and we shared some great laughs before I walked out of Howard. I validated my CTA Park & Ride receipt and went

home. Once at home I made my last video in a CTA uniform called “The Last CTA Dance.” This was a lot of fun to do. When I took my uniform off I felt it. For the last 16 years I did my best to provide our riders with excellent service. I learned so much over these years. One thing is certain:

“I Loved Working At The CTA”

About The Author

-------------   --------------------

Marcus L. Boston worked at the Chicago Transit Authority 16 years. He is now the CEO of Unfazed Publishing in Tampa Florida. Marcus is the author 17 books with many more titles to come, and he's been a Christian for 30 years. Marcus writes books to build up people's lives and he writes books for entertainment purposes. His trademark in writing is being very transparent. He shares his life in truth in an effort to show non-Christians the grace that God has for himself is the same grace God has for them. He shares his failures in an effort to help others avoid the same pitfalls he experienced; especially those who didn't grow up in the church. His personal theme is "Making The Church A Better Place"

44512 BOSTON, MARCUS

My Favorite Mural

This building was demolished. It's now gone.

I passed this mural for years on my trains.

MARCUS L
BOSTON WORLD

UNFAZED PUBLISHING
YOUR MIND IS OUR BUSINESS

Book Me

------------- ----------------

Would you like to book me for an appearance or speaking engagement? Would you like autographed books? Would you like to become an author with me? Please contact me.

info@unfazedpublishing.com

www.UnfazedPublishing.com

www.MarcusLBoston.world

224.762.2242 business only

c

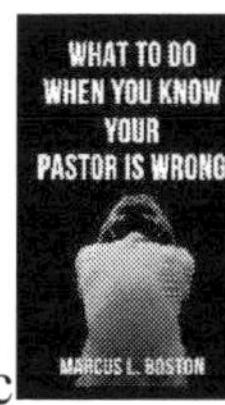

(Kindle Only)

Books Available On

IBooks – Kindle – Amazon

Autographed Copies @
www.MarcusLBoston.world

44512 BOSTON, MARCUS

Made in the USA
Monee, IL
08 July 2024

61495850R10083